AAT

Credit Management

Level 4

Professional Diploma in

Accounting

Question Bank

For assessments from

September 2017

Second edition 2017

ISBN 9781 5097 1268 7

British Library Cataloguing-in-Publication Data
A catalogue record for this book is available from the British Library

Published by

BPP Learning Media Ltd
BPP House, Aldine Place
142-144 Uxbridge Road
London W12 8AA

www.bpp.com/learningmedia

Printed in the United Kingdom

The contents of this course material are intended as a guide and not professional advice. Although every effort has been made to ensure that the contents of this course material are correct at the time of going to press, BPP Learning Media makes no warranty that the information in this course material is accurate or complete and accept no liability for any loss or damage suffered by any person acting or refraining from acting as a result of the material in this course material.

We are grateful to the AAT for permission to reproduce the sample assessment(s). The answers to the sample assessment(s) have been published by the AAT. All other answers have been prepared by BPP Learning Media Ltd.

A note about copyright

Dear Customer

What does the little © mean and why does it matter?

Your market-leading BPP books, course materials and e-learning materials do not write and update themselves. People write them on their own behalf or as employees of an organisation that invests in this activity. Copyright law protects their livelihoods. It does so by creating rights over the use of the content.

Breach of copyright is a form of theft – as well as being a criminal offence in some jurisdictions, it is potentially a serious breach of professional ethics.

With current technology, things might seem a bit hazy but, basically, without the express permission of BPP Learning Media:

- Photocopying our materials is a breach of copyright

- Scanning, ripcasting or conversion of our digital materials into different file formats, uploading them to Facebook or e-mailing them to your friends is a breach of copyright

You can, of course, sell your books, in the form in which you have bought them – once you have finished with them. (Is this fair to your fellow students? We update for a reason.) Please note the e-products are sold on a single user licence basis: we do not supply 'unlock' codes to people who have bought them secondhand.

And what about outside the UK? BPP Learning Media strives to make our materials available at prices students can afford by local printing arrangements, pricing policies and partnerships which are clearly listed on our website. A tiny minority ignore this and indulge in criminal activity by illegally photocopying our material or supporting organisations that do. If they act illegally and unethically in one area, can you really trust them?

BPP
LEARNING MEDIA

Contents

Introduction

This is BPP Learning Media's AAT Question Bank for *Credit Management*. It is part of a suite of ground-breaking resources produced by BPP Learning Media for AAT assessments.

This Question Bank has been written in conjunction with the BPP Course Book, and has been carefully designed to enable students to practise all of the learning outcomes and assessment criteria for the units that make up *Credit Management*. It is fully up to date as at June 2017 and reflects both the AAT's qualification specification and the sample assessment provided by the AAT.

This Question Bank contains these key features:

- Tasks corresponding to each chapter of the Course Book. Some tasks are designed for learning purposes, others are of assessment standard

- AAT's AQ2016 sample assessment and answers for *Credit Management* and further BPP practice assessments

The emphasis in all tasks and assessments is on the practical application of the skills acquired.

VAT

You may find tasks throughout this Question Bank that need you to calculate or be aware of a rate of VAT. This is stated at 20% in these examples and questions.

Approaching the assessment

When you sit the assessment it is very important that you follow the on screen instructions. This means you need to carefully read the instructions, both on the introduction screens and during specific tasks.

When you access the assessment you should be presented with an introductory screen with information similar to that shown below (taken from the introductory screen from one of the AAT's AQ2016 sample assessments for *Credit Management*).

You have **2 hours and 30 minutes** to complete this sample assessment.

This assessment contains **7 tasks** and you should attempt to complete **every** task.
Each task is independent. You will not need to refer to your answers to previous tasks.
Read every task carefully to make sure you understand what is required.

Where the date is relevant, it is given in the task data.
Both minus signs and brackets can be used to indicate negative numbers **unless** task instructions say otherwise.

You must use a full stop to indicate a decimal point. For example, write 100.57 NOT 100,57 or 100 57
You may use a comma to indicate a number in the thousands, but you don't have to. For example 10000 and 10,000 are both acceptable.

The actual instructions will vary depending on the subject you are studying for. It is very important you read the instructions on the introductory screen and apply them in the assessment. You don't want to lose marks when you know the correct answer just because you have not entered it in the right format.

In general, the rules set out in the AAT sample assessments for the subject you are studying for will apply in the real assessment, but you should carefully read the information on this screen again in the real assessment, just to make sure. This screen may also confirm the VAT rate used if applicable.

A full stop is needed to indicate a decimal point. We would recommend using minus signs to indicate negative numbers and leaving out the comma signs to indicate thousands, as this results in a lower number of key strokes and less margin for error when working under time pressure. Having said that, you can use whatever is easiest for you as long as you operate within the rules set out for your particular assessment.

You have to show competence throughout the assessment and you should therefore complete all of the tasks. Don't leave questions unanswered.

In some assessments, written or complex tasks may be human marked. In this case you are given a blank space or table to enter your answer into. You are told in the assessments which tasks these are (note: there may be none if all answers are marked by the computer).

If these involve calculations, it is a good idea to decide in advance how you are going to lay out your answers to such tasks by practising answering them on a word document, and certainly you should try all such tasks in this Question Bank and in the AAT's environment using the sample assessment.

When asked to fill in tables, or gaps, never leave any blank even if you are unsure of the answer. Fill in your best estimate.

Note that for some assessments where there is a lot of scenario information or tables of data provided (eg tax tables), you may need to access these via 'pop-ups'. Instructions will be provided on how you can bring up the necessary data during the assessment.

Finally, take note of any task specific instructions once you are in the assessment. For example you may be asked to enter a date in a certain format or to enter a number to a certain number of decimal places.

Grading

To achieve the qualification and to be awarded a grade, you must pass all the mandatory unit assessments, all optional unit assessments (where applicable) and the synoptic assessment.

The AAT Level 4 Professional Diploma in Accounting will be awarded a grade. This grade will be based on performance across the qualification. Unit assessments and synoptic assessments are not individually graded. These assessments are given a mark that is used in calculating the overall grade.

How overall grade is determined

You will be awarded an overall qualification grade (Distinction, Merit, and Pass). If you do not achieve the qualification you will not receive a qualification certificate, and the grade will be shown as unclassified.

The marks of each assessment will be converted into a percentage mark and rounded up or down to the nearest whole number. This percentage mark is then weighted according to the weighting of the unit assessment or synoptic assessment within the qualification. The resulting weighted assessment percentages are combined to arrive at a percentage mark for the whole qualification.

Grade definition	Percentage threshold
Distinction	90–100%
Merit	80–89%
Pass	70–79%
Unclassified	0–69% Or failure to pass one or more assessment/s

Re-sits

The AAT Professional Diploma In Accounting is not subject to re-sit restrictions.

You should only be entered for an assessment when you are well prepared and you expect to pass the assessment.

AAT qualifications

The material in this book may support the following AAT qualifications:

AAT Professional Diploma in Accounting Level 4, AAT Professional Diploma in Accounting at SCQF Level 8 and Certificate: Accounting (Level 5 AATSA).

Supplements

From time to time we may need to publish supplementary materials to one of our titles. This can be for a variety of reasons. From a small change in the AAT unit guidance to new legislation coming into effect between editions.

You should check our supplements page regularly for anything that may affect your learning materials. All supplements are available free of charge on our supplements page on our website at:

www.bpp.com/learning-media/about/students

Improving material and removing errors

There is a constant need to update and enhance our study materials in line with both regulatory changes and new insights into the assessments.

From our team of authors BPP appoints a subject expert to update and improve these materials for each new edition.

Their updated draft is subsequently technically checked by another author and from time to time non-technically checked by a proof reader.

We are very keen to remove as many numerical errors and narrative typos as we can but given the volume of detailed information being changed in a short space of time we know that a few errors will sometimes get through our net.

We apologise in advance for any inconvenience that an error might cause. We continue to look for new ways to improve these study materials and would welcome your suggestions. If you have any comments about this book, please email nisarahmed@bpp.com or write to Nisar Ahmed, AAT Head of Programme, BPP Learning Media Ltd, BPP House, Aldine Place, London W12 8AA

Question Bank

Chapter 1 – Managing the granting of credit

Task 1.1

Which of the following is a cash transaction?

	✓
Purchase of non-current assets on an instalment basis	
Sale of goods for list price less 2% settlement discount for payment within seven days	
Payment of expenses using a company credit card	
Sale of non-current assets with terms of 30 days for payment	

Task 1.2

There are two main stages of the credit control function – the ordering cycle and the collection cycle.

Consider the following statements:

(i)   A customer receiving an invoice is part of the collection cycle.
(ii)   A customer being offered credit is part of the collection cycle.
(iii)   A statement sent to a customer is part of the ordering cycle.
(iv)   Establishing a customer's credit status is part of the ordering cycle.

The correct statements are:

	✓
(i) and (ii)	
(ii) and (iv)	
(ii) and (iii)	
(i) and (iv)	

Task 1.3

Which of the following stages in the ordering and collection cycle is least likely to represent a responsibility of the credit control function?

	✓
Issuing offer of credit to customer	
Issuing invoice to customer	
Issuing statement to customer	
Issuing payment reminder letter to customer	

Task 1.4

The normal credit terms for a business are that payment should be made within 60 days of the invoice date but a settlement discount of 2% is offered for payment within 14 days of the invoice.

How would this be expressed on the sales invoice to the customer?

	✓
Net 14/60 days	
Gross 60 days net 2% 14 days	
Gross 60 days 2% discount for payment within 14 days	
Net 60 days 2% discount for payment within 14 days	

Task 1.5

Which of the following is not a main role of the credit control department?

	✓
The initial decision whether to grant credit	
Ongoing checks on credit limits	
The pursuit of payment	
The despatch of goods	

Task 1.6

Which of the following is NOT an external source of information for assessing a customer's credit status?

	✓
The internet	
Customer visit	
Companies House (for filed financial statements)	
Bank reference	

Task 1.7

Which of the following would not be classified as a liquid asset?

	✓
Receivables	
Bank deposit accounts	
Non-current assets	
Inventory	

Task 1.8

What are the two main stages in the credit control function?

	✓
Despatch cycle and collection cycle	
Ordering cycle and payment cycle	
Despatch cycle and payment cycle	
Ordering cycle and collection cycle	

Task 1.9

Which of the following describes the liquidity of a business?

	✓
The ability to make a profit	
The ability to pay amounts when they are due	
The ability to raise loan finance	
The ability to pay a dividend when due	

Task 1.10

Which of the following sources of information would be useful in assessing the credit status of a potential new credit customer?

(i)   Bank reference
(ii)   Aged receivables' listing
(iii)   Sales representatives' knowledge
(iv)   Credit agency reference
(v)   Trade reference
(vi)   Analysis of recent financial statements

	✓
(i), (iv), (v) and (vi)	
(ii), (iv), (v) and (vi)	
(i), (iii), (iv) and (v)	
(ii), (iii), (v) and (vi)	

Task 1.11

Which of the following is a credit transaction?

	✓
Purchase of goods by cheque	
Purchase of a non-current asset in three equal instalments	
Sale of goods by credit card	
Delivery of goods to customer for cash	

Task 1.12
Which of the following is correct?

	✓
Despatch of goods is part of the collection cycle.	
The customer being offered credit is part of the collection cycle.	
Establishing customer credit status is part of the ordering cycle.	
A statement sent to a customer is part of the ordering cycle.	

Task 1.13

An organisation has credit terms of 30 days but some customers are offered a 2% discount for payment within 10 days.

How would these credit terms be disclosed on the customer's invoice?

	✓
Gross 30 days net 20 days 2%	
Gross 30 days 2% discount for 10 days	
Net 30 days 2% discount for 10 days	
Net 30 days 2% discount for 20 days	

Task 1.14

Which of the following sources of information would be useful in determining whether to increase the credit period offered to an existing credit customer?

(i)   Bank reference
(ii)   Aged receivables' listing
(iii)   Sales representatives' knowledge
(iv)   Credit agency reference
(v)   Trade reference
(vi)   Analysis of recent financial statements

	✓
(ii), (iii), (iv) and (vi)	
(i), (ii), (v) and (vi)	
(ii), (iii), (v) and (vi)	
(i), (iii), (iv) and (v)	

Chapter 2 – Granting credit to customers

Task 2.1

Which of the following would NOT be a normal method of establishing the creditworthiness of potential new customers?

	✓
Aged receivables' analysis	
Bank reference	
Credit reference agency	
Supplier reference	

Task 2.2

Which of the following are external sources of information about a company requesting credit from your business?

	✓
Supplier reference, credit reference agency, aged receivables' analysis	
Bank reference, aged receivables' analysis, Companies House	
Supplier reference, personal visit, bank reference	
Bank reference, Companies House, credit reference agency	

Task 2.3

Which of the following are valid reasons for deciding not to grant credit to a new customer?

(i) Adverse press reports about the customer
(ii) A non-committal bank reference
(iii) Lack of financial statements due to being a recently started company

	✓
(i) and (ii)	
(i) and (iii)	
(ii) and (iii)	
All of the above	

Task 2.4

A business has a gross profit of £125,000 and an operating profit (profit from operations) of £60,000. The annual revenue was £500,000 and the total net assets of the business were £600,000.

Calculate the following ratios:

Gross profit margin	
Operating profit margin	
Return on capital employed	
Net asset turnover	

Task 2.5

Given below is an extract from the statement of financial position of a business:

	£000	£000
Non-current assets		1,200
Current assets		
Inventory	80	
Trade receivables	120	
Cash	10	
	210	
Current liabilities		
Trade payables	100	
Tax	8	
	108	
Net current assets		102
		1,302
Long-term loans		(500)
		802

The summarised statement of profit or loss for the year is:

	£000
Sales revenue	750
Cost of sales	(500)
Gross profit	250
Operating expenses	(180)
Finance costs (interest paid)	(40)
Profit before tax	30
Tax	(8)
Profit for the year	22

Calculate the following accounting ratios:

Current ratio	
Quick ratio	
Inventory holding period	
Accounts receivable collection period	
Accounts payable payment period	
Return on capital employed	
Gearing ratio	
Interest cover	

Task 2.6

You are the credit controller for a business which has received a request for £20,000 of credit from a potential new customer, Faverly Ltd. Faverly Ltd has provided you with its latest set of financial statements which are summarised as follows:

Statement of profit or loss for the year ended 30 June

	20X8 £000	20X7 £000
Sales revenue	2,400	2,250
Cost of sales	(1,870)	(1,770)
Gross profit	530	480
Operating expenses	(230)	(210)
Operating profit	300	270
Finance costs (interest payable)	(70)	(48)
Profit before tax	230	222
Taxation	(57)	(55)
Profit after tax	173	167

Statements of financial position as at 30 June

	20X8 £000	20X7 £000
ASSETS		
Non-current assets	3,200	2,867
Current assets		
Inventory	264	216
Trade receivables	336	360
	600	576
Total assets	3,800	3,443

	20X8 £000	20X7 £000
EQUITY AND LIABILITIES		
Equity		
Share capital	1,500	1,500
Retained earnings	1,196	1,083
Total equity	2,696	2,583
Current liabilities		
Trade payables	384	380
Bank overdraft	720	480
Total liabilities	1,104	860
Total equity and liabilities	3,800	3,443

You have also received a bank reference from Faverly Ltd's bank which reads 'should prove good for your figures'.

Finally, you have received the following trade references:

We have received a request for credit from Faverly Ltd who have quoted yourselves as a referee. We would be grateful if you could answer the following questions and return in the stamped addressed envelope enclosed.

How long has the customer been trading with you?	Three years six months
Your credit terms with customer per month	£10,000
Period of credit granted	30 days
Payment record	Prompt/occasionally late/slow
Have you ever suspended credit to the customer?	Yes/No
If yes – when and for how long?	20X6 for six months
Any other relevant information	

We have received a request for credit from Faverly Ltd who have quoted yourselves as a referee. We would be grateful if you could answer the following questions and return in the stamped addressed envelope enclosed.

How long has the customer been trading with you?	Five years three months
Your credit terms with customer per month	£10,000
Period of credit granted	30 days
Payment record	Prompt/occasionally late/slow
Have you ever suspended credit to the customer?	Yes/No
Any other relevant information	

You are required to carry out an assessment of the information provided for Faverly Ltd and to record your results and recommendation as to whether credit of £20,000 should be extended to Faverly Ltd in a memo to the finance director of your business.

Task 2.7

You are the credit controller for a business and you have received a request from Fisher Ltd for credit of £15,000 from your company on a 30-day basis. Two trade references have been provided but no bank reference. You have also received the last set of published financial statements which include the previous year's comparative figures.

The trade references appeared satisfactory although one is from Froggett & Sons and it has been noted that the managing director of Fisher Ltd is Mr N Froggett. Analysis of the financial statements has indicated a decrease in profitability during the last year, a high level of gearing and fairly low liquidity ratios.

Draft a letter to the finance director of Fisher Ltd on the basis that credit is to be currently refused but may be extended once the most recent financial statements have been examined.

Task 2.8

Which of the following would be possible reasons for the refusal of credit to a new customer?

(i)   A non-committal or poor bank reference
(ii)   Not having traded with the customer before
(iii)   Concerns about the validity of any trade references submitted
(iv)   Adverse press comment about the potential customer
(v)   Customer is in a different line of business to most customers

	✓
(ii), (iii) and (iv)	
(i), (ii) and (v)	
(i), (iii) and (iv)	
(ii), (iv) and (v)	

Task 2.9

The following statements relate to EBITDA, a figure which is sometimes used in financial analysis calculations:

(i)   EBITDA stands for Earnings before Interest, Tax, Dividends and Amortisation.

(ii)   EBITDA removes some of the subjectivity from the profit figure that arises as a result of management and accounting policies.

Which of the following is the correct description of the accuracy of these statements?

Statement (i)	Statement (ii)	✓
True	False	
True	True	
False	False	
False	True	

Task 2.10

You are employed as an assistant accountant in Fastover Ltd. Your company's financial controller wants you to assess the creditworthiness of Whittle Ltd. Whittle Ltd has placed a large order with your company and any problems paying would have an impact on your company's cash flow.

You have a copy of Fastover Ltd's credit control procedures manual which sets guidelines on when credit should be granted. Extracts are set out below.

Extract from procedures manual

Extending credit to new customers

The supply of goods/services on credit necessarily involves risk. To minimise that risk the following steps should be taken before extending credit to a new customer.

1. Two references from independent referees should be obtained. Any problems raised by the references should be followed-up and further references should be taken, if appropriate.

2. The latest set of financial statements of a company should be obtained and ratio analysis undertaken. Any problems raised by the analysis should be followed-up.

3. Assuming points 1 and 2 are satisfactory, a credit limit should be set by the Credit Control Manager. This should initially be a very conservative limit which is closely monitored. The limit may be reviewed after six months.

BPP
LEARNING MEDIA

You have also received the following references from two of Whittle Ltd's suppliers and extracts from Whittle Ltd's financial statements over the last two years.

FASTOVER LTD

11 Beal Street

Wallington

WL1 9PO

Tel: 0331 8676767

5 January 20X8

PRIVATE AND CONFIDENTIAL

Credit Manager

Greatlygrow Ltd

Long Street

Wallington

WL7 9ZW

Dear Sir or Madam

We have recently received a request from a customer of ours, Whittle Ltd, giving yourselves as a reference. We would be grateful if you would answer the following questions and return them in the enclosed stamped addressed envelope.

1. For how long has Whittle Ltd been trading with you?

    One year

2. Did you take up references for Whittle Ltd when you began trading with them?

    Two references

3. How long a credit period do you normally extend to Whittle Ltd?

    Six weeks

4. Does Whittle Ltd make payments in accordance with credit terms?

    Yes

5. Have you ever suspended credit being extended to Whittle Ltd?

    No

    If YES please give date and period of suspension.

6. Please supply any information which you consider relevant.

Thank you for your help.

Yours faithfully

Brian Herbert

Brian Herbert – Credit Control Manager

FASTOVER LTD
11 Beal Street
Wallington
WL1 9PO
Tel: 0331 8676767

5 January 20X8

PRIVATE AND CONFIDENTIAL

Credit Manager

Weston Ltd

Weston Court

Wallington, WL5 8PP

Dear Sir or Madam

We have recently received a request from a customer of ours, Whittle Ltd, giving yourselves as a reference. We would be grateful if you would answer the following questions and return them in the enclosed stamped addressed envelope.

1. For how long has Whittle Ltd been trading with you?

Five years

2. Did you take up references for Whittle Ltd when you began trading with them?

Two references

3. How long a credit period do you normally extend to Whittle Ltd?

Two months

4. Does Whittle Ltd make payments in accordance with credit terms?

Usually

5. Have you ever suspended credit being extended to Whittle Ltd?

Yes

If YES please give date and period of suspension.

Once, two years ago for six months

6. Please supply any information which you consider relevant.

Thank you for your help.

Yours faithfully

Brian Herbert

Brian Herbert – Credit Control Manager

Extracts from the financial statements of Whittle Ltd
Statements of financial position

	This year £	Last year £
ASSETS		
Non-current assets		
Intangible assets	200	180
Tangible non-current assets	790	670
Investments	900	600
	1,890	1,450
Current assets		
Inventories	200	170
Trade receivables	800	750
Cash	90	105
	1,090	1,025
Total assets	2,980	2,475
EQUITY AND LIABILITIES		
Equity		
Called-up share capital	1,000	1,000
Retained earnings	510	117
Total equity	1,510	1,117
Non-current liabilities		
Borrowings	500	400
Current liabilities		
Trade payables	900	890
Other	70	68
	970	958
Total liabilities	1,470	1,358
Total equity and liabilities	2,980	2,475
Statement of profit or loss extract		
Profit after interest and taxation	500	190

Using the information given and bearing in mind the guidelines in the quality control procedures manual, recommend in a memo to the financial controller whether Whittle Ltd should have credit terms extended to it.

Your ratio analysis should include the following ratios:

- Current ratio
- Quick ratio (or acid test ratio)
- Gearing ratio

Task 2.11

You work as an accounting technician for Sleepy Ltd. You have recently received a request for credit facilities from the finance director of Dreams Ltd. The company has supplied its statement of profit or loss for the year ended 30 June 20X8. In addition, in accordance with the credit policy of Sleepy Ltd, trade references have been obtained from two of Dreams Ltd's suppliers, Carpets Ltd and Wardrobes Ltd. The request for credit, statement of profit or loss and references are as follows.

DREAMS LTD
17 High Street
Newport
South Wales

Mr S Wilks
Financial Controller

Sleepy Ltd
Tregarn Trading Estate
Cardiff
CF1 3EW

21 December 20X8

Dear Mr Wilks

We are a long-established company and trade as a retailer of furniture. We are keen to do business with your company. In order to facilitate this we would be grateful if you could confirm that you will be able to provide us with £20,000 of credit on 60 days terms.

I enclose a copy of our latest audited statement of profit or loss. You may also wish to contact two of our existing suppliers for trade references. I would suggest the following two:

Carpets Ltd
Monnow Way
Bristol
BS7 6TY

Wardrobes Ltd
Pansy Park
Liverpool
L4 1HQ

I look forward to hearing from you shortly.

Yours sincerely

D Jones

David Jones – Finance director

CARPETS LTD
Monnow Way
Bristol
BS7 6TY

Pat King
Accounting Technician
Sleepy Ltd
Tregarn Trading Estate
Cardiff
CF1 3EW

28 December 20X8

Dear Sir/Madam

In response to your request for credit information on Dreams Ltd our response is as follows:

- We have traded with the company for four years.

- We allow the company £10,000 of credit on 30-day terms.

- We find that on average the company takes 60 days to settle their account with us.

- We are not aware of any other information which you should consider.

Yours faithfully

A Evans

Anne Evans – Credit Controller

WARDROBES LTD
Pansy Park
Liverpool
L4 1HQ

Pat King
Accounting Technician
Sleepy Ltd
Tregarn Trading Estate
Cardiff
CF1 3EW

28 December 20X8

Dear Sir/Madam

In response to your request for credit information on Dreams Ltd our response is as follows:

- We have traded with the company for three months.

- We allow the company £2,500 of credit on 30 days terms.

- The company settles its account with us in accordance with our credit terms.

- We are not aware of any other information which you should consider.

Yours faithfully

J Corkhill

J Corkhill – Credit Controller

Dreams Ltd

Statement of profit or loss for the year ended 30 June

	20X8 £000	20X7 £000
Sales revenue	1,800	1,750
Cost of sales	(1,250)	(1,190)
Gross profit	550	560
Net operating expenses	(500)	(550)
Operating profit	50	10
Finance costs	(30)	(20)
Profit/(loss) before taxation	20	(10)
Taxation	–	3
Profit/(loss) for the year after taxation	20	(7)

(a) **Prepare a memo setting out any concerns you have in connection with the request. You should include an analysis of the statement of profit or loss of Dreams Ltd and refer to the trade references.**

(b) **Draft a letter to Mr D Jones at Dreams Ltd in reply to the original request for credit facilities.**

Task 2.12

If the accounts receivable collection period is greater than the accounts payable payment period this will mean which of the following for a business?

	✓
The business is making a profit.	
The business is making a loss.	
Cash is going out of the business more quickly than it is coming in.	
Cash is coming into the business more quickly than it is going out.	

Task 2.13

Consider each of the following statements:

(i)   The granting of credit can result in lost interest to a business.
(ii) The granting of credit can increase sales.
(iii) The granting of credit can decrease irrecoverable debts.

Which of the statements are correct?

	✓
(i) and (ii) only	
(i) and (iii) only	
(ii) and (iii) only	
All three	

Task 2.14

What question would not normally be asked when requesting a trade reference from a supplier of a potential new credit customer?

	✓
Have you ever suspended credit to this customer?	
How long have you been trading with this customer?	
Do you think this customer has a good reputation?	
What level of credit do you allow this customer?	

Task 2.15

A company has a gross profit of £298,000 and an operating profit of £149,000. Share capital is £400,000, reserves total £380,000 and there is a long-term loan of £150,000.

What is the return on capital employed?

	✓
28.1%	
19.1%	
32.0%	
16.0%	

Task 2.16

Which of the following is a disadvantage of management accounts compared to financial accounts as a means of assessing a prospective credit customer?

	✓
They are more up to date.	
They show the information that management feels important.	
They are not in a set format therefore can be tailored to the organisation.	
They are not audited.	

Task 2.17

The use of EBITDA rather than profit before interest when calculating ratios for an organisation has the following advantage.

	✓
The calculation is simpler.	
The figure is a closer approximation to profit.	
The figure gives an idea of the gearing of the organisation.	
The figure gives a closer approximation to cash flow.	

Task 2.18

Which of the following would not be included in a letter of refusal of credit to a potential new credit customer?

	✓
Offer of cash trading	
Offer of future reassessment of creditworthiness	
Details of supplier references	
Concerns about financial statements	

Task 2.19

Identify two tasks that sales representatives could carry out during customer visits that would assist the credit control department in deciding whether to grant or extend credit to customers.

Task 2.20

Pyllon Ltd uses a credit rating system to assess the credit status of new customers. The credit rating (scoring) system below is used to assess the risk of default by calculating key indicators (ratios), comparing them to the table and calculating an aggregate score.

Credit rating (scoring) system	Score	Credit rating (scoring) system	Score
Operating profit margin		**Current ratio**	
Losses	–5	Less than 1	–20
Less than 5%	0	1 and above but less than 1.25	–10
5% and above but less than 10%	5	1.25 and above but less than 1.5	0
10% and above but less than 20%	10	1.5 or more	10
20% or more	20	**Gearing (total debt/total debt plus equity)**	
Interest cover		Less than 25%	20
No cover	–30	25% and above but less than 50%	10
Less than 1	–20	50% and above but less than 65%	0
1 and above but less than 2	–10	65% and above but less than 75%	–20
2 and above but less than 4	0	75% and above but less than 80%	–40
4 or more	10	80% or more	–100

Risk	Aggregate score
Very low risk	Between 60 and 21
Low risk	Between 20 and 1
Medium risk	Between 0 and –24
High risk	Between –25 and –50
Very high risk	Between –51 and –160

The sales department has asked for a credit limit of £50,000 to be given to Ultra Ltd, a potential new customer. The financial information below has been supplied by Ultra Ltd.

Ultra Ltd statement of profit or loss	20X6 £000	20X5 £000
Sales revenue	6,340	7,590
Cost of sales	4,650	5,720
Gross profit	**1,690**	**1,870**
Distribution costs	337	463
Administration expenses	776	1,153
Operating profit	**577**	**254**
Finance costs	170	180
Profit/(loss) before taxation	**407**	**74**
Taxation	81	15
Profit/(loss) for the year	**326**	**59**

Ultra Ltd statement of financial position	20X6 £000	20X5 £000
Assets		
Non-current assets		
Property, plant and equipment	1,960	5,203
Current assets		
Inventories	44	17
Trade and other receivables	950	705
Cash	2,360	1,020
	3,354	**1,742**
Total assets	**5,314**	**6,945**
Equity and liabilities		
Equity		
Share capital	1,500	1,500
Retained earnings	538	212
Total Equity	**2,038**	**1,712**
Non-current liabilities		
Borrowing	2,000	3,000
Current liabilities		
Borrowing	222	233
Trade and other payables	1,054	2,000
Total liabilities	**3,276**	**5,233**
Total equity and liabilities	**5,314**	**6,945**

(a) **Complete the table below by calculating the key indicators (to two decimal places) for 20X5 and 20X4 for Ultra Ltd, and rate the company using the credit rating scoring system.**

Ultra Ltd	20X6 Indicator	20X6 Rating	20X5 Indicator	20X5 Rating
Operating profit margin %				
Interest cover				
Current ratio				
Gearing %				
Total credit rating				

Rating	Decision
Very low or low risk current year and very low or low risk previous year	Accept
Very low or low risk current year and medium risk previous year	Accept
Very low or low risk current year and high or very high risk previous year	Request latest management accounts and defer decision
Very high risk or high risk current year	Reject
Medium risk current year and medium, low or very low risk previous year	Accept
Medium risk current year and high or very high risk previous year	Request latest management accounts and defer decision

(b)   **Based on the results of your credit rating and using the table above, recommend whether the requested credit limit should be given to Ultra Ltd.**

Customer	Decision
Ultra Ltd	▼

Picklist:

Accept
Reject
Request latest management accounts and defer decision

Chapter 3 – Legislation and credit control

Task 3.1

What are the three fundamental elements of a contract?

	✓
Consideration, offer, acceptance	
Intention to create legal relations, consideration, agreement	
Invitation to treat, offer, acceptance	
Offer, acceptance, intention to create legal relations	

Task 3.2

Ashley goes into a shop and picks up a newspaper and goes to the cash till to pay for it.

What element of the contract is this?

	✓
Invitation to treat	
Consideration	
Offer	
Acceptance	

Task 3.3

In contract law an offer can be brought to an end in a variety of different ways.

Which of the following are ways in which an offer can be brought to an end?

(i)   Revocation of the offer
(ii)   Legal action
(iii)   A counter-offer
(iv)   Lapse of set period of time
(v)   Silence

	✓
(i), (iii) and (iv)	
(ii), (iii) and (v)	
(i), (iii) and (v)	
(i), (iv) and (v)	

Task 3.4

A term in a contract is fundamental to the contract and if it is broken then the party breaking the term will be in breach of contract and can be sued for damages and the injured party can terminate the contract if they wish.

What is the name given to this type of term?

	✓
Express term	
Implied term	
Warranty	
Condition	

Task 3.5

There are a variety of possible remedies for a breach of contract.

Which of these remedies is most appropriate for a seller of goods where the buyer has not paid?

	✓
Monetary damages	
Action for the price	
Specific performance	
Injunction	

Task 3.6

An action is to be brought to court against a receivable for non-payment of an amount of £7,500.

Which court should the action be brought in?

	✓
Crown Court	
High Court	
Employment Tribunal	
County Court	

Task 3.7

A business is owed £20,000 from a receivable and the court has ordered a warrant of execution.

What is a warrant of execution?

	✓
The business will be paid the amount owing directly by the receivable's employer as a certain amount is deducted from their weekly/monthly pay.	
The business will be paid directly by a third party.	
A court bailiff seizes and sells the receivable's goods on behalf of the business.	
The receivable makes regular, agreed payments into court to pay off the debt.	

Task 3.8

What is a statutory demand?

	✓
A method of payment similar to a standing order	
A demand for payment from an outstanding receivable of £5,000 or more	
A demand from the tax authorities for payment	
A demand for payment of interest on outstanding amounts for a receivable	

Task 3.9

If a customer is declared bankrupt what is the order in which their assets are used to make payments due?

	✓
Secured creditors, unsecured creditors, bankruptcy costs, preferential creditors	
Preferential creditors, secured creditors, bankruptcy costs, unsecured creditors	
Preferential creditors, secured creditors, unsecured creditors, bankruptcy costs	
Secured creditors, bankruptcy costs, preferential creditors, unsecured creditors	

Task 3.10

In a liquidation, a company is dissolved and the assets are realised with debts being paid out of the proceeds and any excess being returned to the shareholders.

In this process by what term are the trade payables of the liquidated business known as?

	✓
Secured creditors with floating charge	
Preferential creditors	
Unsecured creditors	
Secured creditors with fixed charge	

Task 3.11

A company is insolvent when it cannot pay its debts as they fall due.

Which of the following is not a route for a payable to recover the amounts due?

	✓
Administration	
Bankruptcy	
Receivership	
Liquidation	

Task 3.12

Under the Data Protection Act what is meant by a data subject?

	✓
A person who holds personal information	
A company whose data is held	
A person who processes personal information	
An individual whose data is held	

Task 3.13

Under the Consumer Rights Act goods are expected to be 'fit for purpose'.

What is meant by 'fit for purpose'?

	✓
They are fully functioning.	
They are of satisfactory quality.	
They are what they are described to be.	
They do what they are expected to do.	

Task 3.14

What is the correct formula for calculating interest under the Late Payment of Commercial Debts Act?

	✓
Net Debt × (base rate + 8%)/365	
Net Debt × (base rate + 8%) × (No. of days overdue/365)	
Gross Debt × (base rate + 8%)/365	
Gross Debt × (base rate + 8%) × (No. of days overdue/365)	

Task 3.15

There are three tracks for recovering debts in the County Court. Which of the following is not a track?

	✓
Multi-track	
Fast track	
Slow track	
Small claims track	

Task 3.16

Which of the following statements is correct?

(i)   The parties to a social or domestic arrangement are presumed to have intended the arrangement to be legally enforceable.

(ii)   The parties to a commercial transaction are presumed not to have intended the arrangement to be legally enforceable.

	✓
(i) only	
(ii) only	
Both (i) and (ii)	
Neither (i) nor (ii)	

Task 3.17

Which of the following statements is correct?

Consideration:

(i)   Must be of adequate and sufficient value

(ii)   Must come from the promisee

	✓
(i) only	
(ii) only	
Both (i) and (ii)	
Neither (i) or (ii)	

Task 3.18

Which of the following is an offer?

	✓
An advertisement in the newsagent's window	
An invitation to tender	
An auction bid	
An exhibition of goods for sale	

Task 3.19

Which of the following are essential requirements of a contract?

(i)   Offer and acceptance
(ii)   Consideration
(iii)   Written contractual terms
(iv)   Intention to create legal relations

	✓
(i), (ii), (iii) and (iv)	
(i), (ii) and (iii)	
(i), (ii) and (iv)	
(i), (iii) and (iv)	

Task 3.20

Which one of the following types of term is stated in a contract and is binding on both parties?

	✓
Express terms	
Implied terms	
Allowed terms	
Intended terms	

Task 3.21

Under the Data Protection Act how many principles of good practice are there?

	✓
5	
8	
10	
12	

Task 3.22

Alexander wrote to Brian and offered to sell him his set of antique cigarette cards for £300. Brian wrote back that he accepted the offer and would pay for them in two instalments of £150.

Is there a contract?

	✓
Yes. There is offer, acceptance and consideration. The contract is valid.	
No. Alexander's letter was not an offer but an invitation to treat.	
No. Until Alexander receives Brian's letter, the acceptance is not valid.	
No. Brian's letter has varied the terms and so is a counter-offer, rejecting Alexander's original offer.	

Task 3.23

Consider the following statements:

(i)   The parties to a social or domestic agreement are presumed to have intended the agreement to be legally enforceable.

(ii) The parties to a commercial agreement are presumed to have intended the arrangement to be legally enforceable.

Which statements are true?

	✓
(i) only	
(ii) only	
Both (i) and (ii)	
Neither statement	

Task 3.24

Which of the following best describes consideration?

	✓
The promise of an exchange of value	
The payment of cash	
The intention for the parties to be legally bound	
The creation of a fair contract	

Task 3.25

Karen orders 5 pairs of running tights from an online sports retailer. The tights are described as 100% polyester. When the tights arrive, Karen checks the labels and sees that the material is described as 60% polyester, 40% elastane.

The contract between Karen and the sports retailer is voidable due to:

	✓
Unfair Contract	
Fraud	
Misrepresentation	
Consumer Credit	

Task 3.26

Will owes Alex £25,000 excluding VAT, which is charged at the standard rate. The debt has been overdue for 90 days. The current Bank of England base rate is 0.5%.

What is the amount of interest that Alex may charge Will under the Late Payment of Commercial Debts (Interest) Act? Calculate your answer to the nearest penny.

£ [   ]

Task 3.27

Identify whether the following statements about the Data Protection Act are true or false.

	True ✓	False ✓
Data cannot be kept for more than six months.		
Individuals have a right to object to decisions taken where there is no human involvement.		
An internet company that wishes to use data collected from individuals for marketing purposes must have the permission of those individuals.		
Information gathered by using CCTV security cameras is not subject to the Data Protection Act rules.		

Task 3.28

Drag and drop the correct words into the following statement.

A retention of title clause within a contract is [   ] . It allows the

supplier to [   ] ownership of the goods supplied. An official receiver

[   ] seek the authority of an insolvency practitioner before

deciding that a claim is valid. If an official receiver sells goods that are subject to a valid retention of title claim by the supplier he or she [   ] liable to pay damages to the supplier.

implicit	can be	transfer	does not have to

| expressly stated | has to | retain | cannot be |

Task 3.29

Creditors have several options to enforce a county court judgement. Match each option to the explanation by clicking on the left box first then on the corresponding right box. You can remove a line by clicking on it.

Enforcement option

| Garnishee Order |

| Charging Order |

| Attachment of earnings |

Explanation

An order issued by a court entitling a creditor to collect payment from the customer of their debtor.

An order issued by a County Court entitling the creditor to instruct a court employee to collect assets from the debtor.

An order issued by a court entitling the creditor to be paid the amount owing directly by the customer's employer, as a certain amount is deducted from their weekly/monthly pay.

An order issued by a court entitling the creditor to enter the premises of the debtor to seize assets to the value of the debt.

An order issued by a court entitling a creditor to receive payment on the sale of specified property.

Chapter 4 – Methods of credit control

Task 4.1

A business has normal credit terms of payment within 60 days of the invoice date. It is considering offering a settlement discount of 1% for payment within 10 days of the invoice date.

Using the simple method what is the approximate annual cost of this discount?

	✓
1%	
0.74%	
7.4%	
73.7%	

Task 4.2

Widmerpool Ltd makes sales to certain customers of £100,000 with an average collection period of two months. Kenneth, its managing director, is considering whether to introduce a discount of 3% on sales to these customers in return for immediate cash settlement. Widmerpool normally requires a 15% return on its investments.

What is the cost of the discount and would it be worth introducing?

Cost	Introduce or not?	✓
18.8%	Yes	
3.8%	Yes	
18.8%	No	
3.8%	No	

Task 4.3

Brickwood grants credit terms of 60 days net to its major customers, but offers an early settlement discount of 2.5% for payment within 7 days.

Using the simple method what is the cost of the discount?

	✓
17.7%	
17.2%	
15.6%	
2.5%	

Task 4.4

Herbage Ltd is proposing to increase the credit period it gives to customers from one calendar month to two calendar months in order to increase revenue from the present annual figure of £18 million. The price of the product is £10 and it costs £6.40 to make. The increase in the credit period is likely to generate an extra 60,000 unit sales per year. The bank interest cost to the company is 15%.

What is the total financing cost of this policy?

	✓
£24,000	
£240,000	
£1,500,000	
£1,600,000	

Task 4.5

Which of the following is not a service provided by a debt factor?

	✓
Administration of the receivables ledger	
Despatch of goods	
Advance of funds	
Insurance against irrecoverable debts	

Task 4.6

Consider the following statements:

(i)   Invoice discounting is where the book value of the company's receivables are advanced to the company.

(ii)   Under an invoice discounting agreement the company collects the debts itself and repays the invoice discounter out of the proceeds.

Which statements are true:

	✓
(i) only	
(ii) only	
(i) and (ii)	
Neither statement	

Task 4.7

Invoice discounting is a method where:

	✓
A business offers a discounted price for goods to customers who buy in bulk	
A business offers a discounted price for customers who pay invoices early	
A business offers a discounted price to customers who buy sub-standard goods	
A business lends money to a customer based on a discounted value of the invoices that customer has issued	

Task 4.8

The purpose of credit insurance is to allow a business to:

	✓
Claim back the legal costs of any court proceedings brought against it by its creditors	
Claim back amounts owed to it by customers who have defaulted	
Claim back the costs of employing temporary staff to undertake debt collection in the event that the credit controller is on long-term sick leave	
Continue to meet the interest payments on its loans in the event that it becomes loss-making	

Task 4.9

80% of the receivables of a business have been insured for their entire amount and any claim on these receivables would be paid in full.

What type of insurance policy is this?

	✓
Annual aggregate excess policy	
Partial turnover policy	
Specific receivables policy	
Whole turnover policy	

Task 4.10

Consider the following statements:

(i)   A credit collection agency is a commercial organisation providing background information and credit status information about companies and individuals.

(ii)   A credit collection agency advances a certain percentage of the carrying amount (book value) of receivables to a business and then takes over the collection of those receivables.

Which of the following correctly describes the accuracy of the statements?

Statement (i)	Statement (ii)	✓
True	True	
True	False	
False	True	
False	False	

Task 4.11

Consider the following statements regarding factoring services:

(i)   With recourse factoring means that the factor bears the risk of irrecoverable debts.

(ii)   Factoring is viewed as a normal business operation and will not affect the relationship between the business and its credit customers.

Which of the statements is true?

	✓
(i) only	
(ii) only	
Both statements	
Neither statement	

Task 4.12

A business currently trades on 30-day credit terms but is considering offering a settlement discount of 1.5% for payment within 14 days of the invoice date.

Using the simple method what is the annual cost of this settlement discount and if the company's bank interest cost is 6% would it be worthwhile to offer the discount?

Cost	Worthwhile	✓
3.5%	Yes	
3.5%	No	
34.7%	Yes	
34.7%	No	

Task 4.13

How do debt collection agencies normally charge for their services?

	✓
A flat fee up front	
A monthly flat rate fee	
A percentage of amounts collected	
A percentage of total receivables	

Task 4.14

The provision of finance by a factoring service is a costly but useful service for a business.

Which of the following are likely costs of this provision of finance service?

(i)   Additional interest charged by suppliers on overdue amounts
(ii)   Service charge
(iii)   Cost of running the receivables ledger
(iv)   Additional interest on bank overdraft
(v)   Interest charge on amounts outstanding

	✓
(i), (ii) and (v)	
(i), (iv) and (v)	
(ii), (iii) and (iv)	
(ii), (iii) and (v)	

Task 4.15

Which of the following is a disadvantage of using the services of a factor?

	✓
Cost savings in receivables ledger	
Cash advance	
Re-instigating receivables ledger	
Irrecoverable debt insurance	

Task 4.16

Under a whole turnover policy of credit insurance which of the following would be true?

	✓
Half of all receivables are covered by the policy.	
Irrecoverable debts are insured above an agreed limit.	
Specific receivables are insured.	
About 80% of receivables are covered for their entire amount.	

Task 4.17

A business currently trades on a basis of one-month credit terms to credit customers. However, the business wishes to increase sales and profits and is considering increasing its credit terms to two months. Currently, the receivables figure of the business is £25,000 and revenue is £300,000. It is anticipated that revenue will increase to £390,000. The business has a net profit percentage of 10% on its sales.

What is the net cash effect as a result of this change?

	✓
£25,000 increase in cash	
£25,000 reduction in cash	
£50,000 increase in cash	
£50,000 reduction in cash	

Task 4.18

A business currently trades on 60-day credit terms but is considering offering a settlement discount of 3% for payment within 14 days of the invoice date.

Using the compound interest method what is the annual cost of this settlement discount?

	✓
3.0%	
80.6%	
18.8%	
27.34%	

Task 4.19

Which of the following are the three main services provided by a factoring service?

(i)   Legal advice
(ii)   Receivables ledger administration
(iii)   Discounting service
(iv)   Provision of finance
(v)   Insurance against irrecoverable debts

	✓
(i), (iv) and (v)	
(i), (iii) and (iv)	
(ii), (iii) and (v)	
(ii), (iv) and (v)	

Task 4.20

Consider the following statements regarding factoring services:

(i)   If a factor administers the receivables ledger then the factor will be responsible for assessing the credit status of customers.

(ii)   Without recourse factoring means that the business not the factor bears the risk of irrecoverable debts.

Which statements are true?

	✓
(i) only	
(ii) only	
Both statements	
Neither statement	

Task 4.21

KWN Ltd is considering alternative ways of managing debt collection. KWNs total receivables ledger balance as at 31 December 20X6 is £3,640,000, which includes £250,000 of debts which are over 90 days.

SNN Co can provide KWN with a facility whereby SNN manages the receivables ledger on behalf of KWN. SNN will lend KWN a maximum of £2,100,000 or 70% of the outstanding receivables balance excluding debts over 90 days. SNN will not provide any protection against irrecoverable debts.

Complete the following sentences.

SNN is offering [▼].

KWN can borrow: £ [ ]

Picklist:

a non-recourse factoring facility
a non-recourse invoice discounting facility
a recourse factoring facility
a recourse invoice discounting facility

Task 4.22

The Sales Manager of Wallace Ltd has found that her sales staff do not understand the annual percentage cost of the early settlement discounts that the company offers to customers.

Complete the following email explaining the early settlement discounts offered by the company.

Email

To: Sales Staff   **Date:** Today

From: AAT Technician   **Subject:** Early Settlement Discounts

Please find below my explanation of how an annual percentage cost of an early settlement discount is calculated.

The effective rate of interest

If a customer pays promptly to take advantage of a 3% early settlement discount, we will receive 97% of the invoice total. This means that the discount we are giving the customer is [▼] of the amount they pay us. This is what it costs us to receive the cash earlier than our normal credit terms. It is called the effective rate of interest.

Discount periods

If the normal credit terms require customers to pay within 30 days of receiving an invoice, and the discount applies if the customer pays within 14 days, we are offering the discount in return for paying 16 days earlier than our normal terms. There are [▼] discount periods of 16 days in a 365 day year.

Annual percentage cost of the early settlement discount using simple interest rates

The annual percentage cost is found by [▼] the effective rate of interest and the discount periods in a year. The annual percentage cost of offering 3% discount to customers paying within 14 days rather than 30 days is [▼] to the nearest whole percent. I trust this will help you in any discussions with customers about early settlement discounts.

AAT Technician

Picklist:

adding
multiplying
square rooting
3%
3.09%
97%
96.91%
100%
12.17
22.81
26.07
29
68
70

Chapter 5 – Managing the supply of credit

Task 5.1

What is a credit customer's credit limit?

	✓
The maximum amount the customer can buy on credit each month	
The maximum amount of each invoice for goods on credit	
The maximum amount the customer can buy on credit each year	
The maximum amount allowed to be outstanding at any point in time	

Task 5.2

A customer of your business has an outstanding balance on its receivables ledger account of £24,519 at 31 July. This balance is made up as follows:

		£
10 May	Inv 042644	1,473
25 May	Inv 042712	3,265
6 June	Inv 042785	4,273
25 June	Inv 042846	4,175
6 July	Credit note 02764	(400)
10 July	Inv 042913	4,463
16 July	Inv 042962	3,143
25 July	Inv 042987	4,127
		24,519

The customer's name is Knightly Ltd and the company has a credit limit of £30,000.

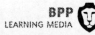

Complete the aged receivables' analysis given below for this customer as at 31 July.

	Total £	Credit limit £	Current, < 30 days £	31–60 days £	61–90 days £	> 90 days £

Task 5.3

Given below is an extract from an aged receivables' analysis for your business at 31 August.

	Total £	Credit limit £	Current < 30 days £	31–60 days £	61–90 days £	> 90 days £
Jeremy Ltd	8,236	10,000	3,757	3,589		890
Lenter Ltd	5,378	8,000	1,873	1,967	1,538	
Friday Partners	400	4,000			400	
Diamond & Co	6,256	5,000	4,227	2,029		

What does the aged receivables' analysis indicate for each of these customers and what action, if any, should be taken?

Task 5.4

You are working in Paddington Ltd's credit control section. The sales manager has asked for your views on the credit status of four organisations to whom Paddington Ltd supplies goods.

Using the extracts from the aged receivables' analysis given below, analyse these four accounts and write a memorandum to the sales manager.

Your memorandum should:

(a)   Provide an opinion of the creditworthiness of the customer and the status of the account

(b)   Suggest how the account should be managed in the future

Extract from: Aged receivables' analysis

Customer name and address	Total due £	Up to 30 days £	Up to 60 days £	Up to 90 days £	Over 90 days £
Megacorp plc, Oakham,					
Rutland	72,540	21,250	12,250	15,500	23,540
Credit limit £85,000					
Terms of sale: 60 days net					
Goodfellows Cycles Ltd,					
Manchester	24,000	19,000			5,000
Credit limit £50,000					
Terms of sale: 30 days net					
Hooper-bikes Ltd, Sheffield	26,750	6,250	9,875	5,275	5,350
Credit limit £25,000					
Terms of sale: 60 days net					
Dynamo Cycles Ltd					
Nottingham	2,750	2,750			
Credit limit £7,500					
Terms of sale: 30 days net					

Task 5.5

Given below is the credit control policy for a business and an extract from its aged receivables' analysis at 30 September.

Credit control policy

1. Invoices must be issued on the same day as goods are despatched.

2. An aged analysis of trade receivables is to be produced monthly.

3. Credit terms are strictly 30 days from the date of invoice.

4. Statements are despatched on the first working day of each month.

5. A reminder letter must be sent when a debt is 14 days overdue.

6. A telephone call to chase payment must be made when a debt is 21 days overdue.

7. The customer will be placed on the stop list when the amount owing is 30 days overdue and a meeting arranged with the customer to discuss the operation of the account.

8. A letter threatening legal action will be sent when the debt is 45 days overdue.

9. Legal proceedings are to be commenced when a debt is 60 days overdue subject to the agreement of the finance director.

Aged receivables' analysis at 30 September: extract

	Total £	Credit limit £	Current < 30 days £	31–60 days £	61–90 days £	> 90 days £
Carnford Ltd	12,430	15,000				12,430
Luxford Ltd	3,400	4,000	2,500	720		180
KLP Ltd	1,560	2,000		600	960	
Flanders Ltd	18,450	20,000	10,240	6,225	1,985	

For each receivable:

• **Set out the action to be taken with regard to the customer account.**

• **State how discussion should be conducted if the account is overdue.**

• **Recommend whether any allowances for doubtful debts are required.**

Task 5.6

Draft a first reminder letter to a customer whose debt of £1,350.46 is 14 days overdue.

The customer's name is Harvey Ltd and its account number is 204764.

Task 5.7

Draft a letter to a customer whose debt of £976.80 is 30 days overdue and who is to be placed on your business's stop list.

The customer's name is Bart & Sons and its account number is B245.

Task 5.8

What is the relevance of the 80/20 rule when dealing with credit control?

	✓
Only 80% of receivables' accounts need to considered when analysing the aged receivables listing.	
Only the first 80 customers on the aged receivables' listing need to be analysed.	
If 20% of the largest customers are analysed this should account for 80% in value.	
It is likely that 20% of debts will need to be written off or an allowance made.	

Task 5.9

You are working in the credit control department of Manton Ltd. An extract from the company's aged receivables' analysis at 30 September 20X7, together with information on the transactions that took place during October, is shown below.

Prepare an aged receivables' analysis as at 31 October 20X7.

Manton Ltd Aged Receivables' Analysis – 30 September 20X7

Credit terms: 30 days

Customer name and ref	Total amount	Current (< 1 month)	Outstanding 1–2 months	Outstanding 2–3 months	Outstanding > 3 months
New Milton	£9,000	£2,000 M89			£7,000 M17
Sway	£1,000	£1,000 M81			
Mudeford	£2,500				£2,500 M24
Barton	£23,000		£13,000 M69	£10,000 M33	
Boscombe	£3,000			£3,000 M38	
TOTAL	**£38,500**	**£3,000**	**£13,000**	**£13,000**	**£9,500**

Transactions during October 20X7:

New Milton	Invoices M17 £7,000 and M89 £2,000 remain unpaid. Invoice M98 £4,000 issued.
Sway	Invoice M81 £1,000 remains unpaid.
Mudeford	Invoice M24 £2,500 paid.
Barton	Paid invoice M33 £10,000. Invoice M69 £13,000 remains unpaid. Invoice M101 £4,000 issued.
Boscombe	Paid invoice M38 £3,000. Invoice M103 £5,000 issued.

Task 5.10

Which of the following is the best explanation of materiality in the context of analysing and chasing outstanding debts?

	✓
Overdue debts under a certain amount should always be ignored.	
Largest debts should be pursued as a first priority with smallest amounts pursued last.	
Debts from significant customers should not be chased in such a way as to damage the relationship with the customer.	
Outstanding debts that are below a certain limit should be written off without attempts to chase them.	

Task 5.11

Frame Ltd's credit controller was sacked recently for failing to implement the company's credit control policies. On analysing the aged receivables you find that Jines Ltd, a customer of Frame Ltd, has not purchased any goods for the last three months and has an amount outstanding of £450 on the receivables ledger.

What action is the most appropriate for you to take in respect of Jines Ltd's debt?

	✓
Telephone Jines Ltd to enquire about the situation in order to determine whether there is any query regarding the amount outstanding and to agree steps for payment.	
Send Jines Ltd a statement and wait for payment.	
Suggest that the accounts department writes off Jines Ltd's debt as it is more than 90 days old.	
Initiate County Court proceedings to recover the debt.	

Task 5.12

A customer's outstanding balance at 30 June 20X9 has been analysed as follows:

19/04/X9	Invoice 17563	2,610
23/05/X9	Invoice 17772	1,667
01/06/X9	Credit note 4612	(331)
10/06/X9	Invoice 17890	1,890
21/06/X9	Invoice 17999	1,560
		7,396

The customer has credit terms of 30 days for payment.

What is the total of the amount that is overdue?

	✓
£1,667	
£2,610	
£3,119	
£4,277	

Task 5.13

Which of the following is correct?

	✓
An irrecoverable debt is one which may or may not be received.	
An irrecoverable debt is written off and does not appear in the statement of financial position.	
A doubtful debt will likely be paid.	
A doubtful debt is written off and does not appear in the statement of financial position.	

Task 5.14

Which of the following would not be part of an organisation's credit control policy?

	✓
Setting of credit limits	
Inventory ordering	
Assessment of credit standing	
Collection procedures	

Task 5.15

Which of the following information would be required in order to open an account for a new credit customer?

(i)   Credit limit agreed
(ii)   Customer's name and address
(iii)   Customer's bank name and address
(iv)   Managing director's name and address
(v)   Payment terms agreed

	✓
(I), (II) and (Iv)	
(ii), (iii) and (v)	
(i), (ii) and (v)	
(ii), (iii) and (v)	

Task 5.16

A customer has a credit limit of £10,000.

What does this mean?

	✓
The customer can spend £10,000 a year on credit.	
The customer can spend £10,000 a month on credit.	
A single order must not exceed £10,000.	
At any point in time the customer's balance must not exceed £10,000.	

Task 5.17

Why is it important that a customer's credit limit should not be exceeded?

	✓
It is a breach of contract.	
It could result in an irrecoverable debt.	
Settlement discounts could be cancelled.	
Sales may be lost.	

Task 5.18

A customer's outstanding balance at 30 June 20X9 has been analysed as follows:

19/04/X9	Invoice 17563	2,610
23/05/X9	Invoice 17772	1,667
01/06/X9	Credit note 4612	(331)
10/06/X9	Invoice 17890	1,890
21/06/X9	Invoice 17999	1,560
		7,396

What is the amount that would appear in the aged receivables analysis as owing between 0–30 days?

	✓
£1,667	
£2,279	
£3,450	
£3,119	

Task 5.19

When analysing receivables balances it is generally believed that 80% of the value of receivables is owed by just 20% of the credit customers.

What is this rule known as?

	✓
80% rule	
20% rule	
80/20 rule	
20/80 rule	

Task 5.20

It is important to distinguish between a doubtful debt and an irrecoverable debt.

Consider the following statements:

(i)   A doubtful debt will never be received and does not appear in the statement of financial position.

(ii) A doubtful debt may be received but does not appear in the statement of financial position.

Which of the statements are true?

	✓
(i) only	
(ii) only	
Both statements	
Neither statement	

Task 5.21

Which of the following would be typical entries into a receivables' ledger account for a credit customer?

(i)   Invoices sent out
(ii)   Statement balances sent out
(iii)   Payments received
(iv)   Order totals received

	✓
(i) and (ii)	
(i) and (iii)	
(ii) and (iii)	
(iii) and (iv)	

Task 5.22

A customer places an order for £5,000 which means that the balance on the customer's receivables' ledger will be £15,000 whereas the credit limit for this customer is £12,000.

What action would be required?

	✓
Despatch the goods to the customer	
Put a stop on the customer's account	
Discuss the situation with the customer	
Make an allowance for a doubtful debt	

Task 5.23

A customer's outstanding balance at 30 June 20X9 has been analysed as follows:

19/04/X9	Invoice 17563	2,610
23/05/X9	Invoice 17772	1,667
01/06/X9	Credit note 4612	(331)
10/06/X9	Invoice 17890	1,890
21/06/X9	Invoice 17999	1,560
		7,396

What is the amount that would appear in the aged receivables' analysis as owing between 61 and 90 days?

	✓
£1,667	
£4,277	
£2,610	
£3,119	

Task 5.24

Analysing the aged receivables' listing should give an indication about a number of factors about a credit customer.

Which of the following could not be determined from an analysis of the aged receivables listing?

	✓
Credit limit exceeded	
Slow payers	
Customer in liquidation	
Old amounts outstanding but recent debts cleared	

Task 5.25

Which of the following would be classified as an irrecoverable debt?

	✓
An amount owing from a customer over which there is a dispute which is being discussed with the customer	
An amount owing from a customer over which there is a dispute and legal proceedings have been instigated	
An amount owing from a customer who has not answered the telephone, replied to letters and is no longer at their trading address	
An amount owing from a customer who has gone into liquidation	

Task 5.26

Which of the following conditions must have been met for a business to successfully claim VAT Bad Debt Relief from HMRC?

	✓
The customer must have ceased trading and not paid one or more invoices due to the business.	
Ownership of the items invoiced must have been transferred to the customer.	
The business making the claim must have written the debt off as bad (irrecoverable).	
The debt must be at least 12 months old.	

Task 5.27

Scott has received a letter from the liquidator of Nicol Ltd. The liquidator has indicated that all unsecured creditors of Nicol will receive a dividend of 2.5p in the pound (£) later in the year. Scott is owed £10,500 by Nicol.

Calculate the amount that Scott should write off as an irrecoverable debt. Ignore VAT. Show your answer to the nearest penny.

£	

Task 5.28

Conic Ltd supplies sportswear and nutritional products to sports retailers. VAT is charged at zero rate on the supply of nutritional products; however, other items are charged at standard rate.

Credit insurance is provided on certain specified accounts only. Conic includes a simple retention of title clause as part of its standard terms of trade.

Conic's standard terms of payment are 30 days from the invoice date. Today's date is 31 December 20X5.

You work in the credit control department of Conic. Your supervisor is away on holiday and is not contactable, however you have been provided with the information below on Lomond, a regular customer of Conic.

Review the information provided for Lomond and prepare comments and an action plan for dealing with the outstanding amounts due to Conic. Your action plan should include a summary of the options available to Conic to pursue outstanding amounts, along with recommendations for provisions or write off of irrecoverable debts where appropriate.

Lomond

Conic delivered nutritional products worth £20,000 and sportswear invoiced at £120,000 to Lomond on 28th December. Conic has just received a telephone call from a member of the credit circle to inform them that a receiver was appointed at Lomond yesterday. Lomond is credit insured for 80% of any unrecovered debt.

Task 5.29

Connoly has an outstanding invoice for £15,000, including VAT due to Pyllon. The invoice is dated 1st March 20X5, payment terms are 30 days from the invoice date. Today is 30 June 20X5. Connoly has often been slow to pay in the past, and has now given several excuses to delay payment, ranging from being unable to trace any of the original documentation to the authorised cheque signatory being away. Pyllon has supplied Connoly with copies of all relevant documentation and, in accordance with the credit control policy, is now about to instruct a debt collection agency or commence legal action.

The HR director has asked you to refrain from sending the debt collectors or instructing solicitors because the Managing Director of Connoly is president of the local tennis club. She wishes to join this club, and she is concerned that any unpleasant tension will affect her application.

Prepare comments and an action plan for dealing with the outstanding amounts due to Pyllon.

Answer Bank

Chapter 1

Task 1.1

The correct answer is: Payment of expenses using a company credit card

A credit card payment is a form of cash payment.

Task 1.2

The correct answer is: (i) and (iv)

Task 1.3

The correct answer is: Issuing invoice to customer

Task 1.4

The correct answer is: Net 60 days 2% discount for payment within 14 days

Task 1.5

The correct answer is: The despatch of goods

Task 1.6

The correct answer is: Customer visit

Task 1.7

The correct answer is: Non-current assets

Task 1.8

The correct answer is: Ordering cycle and collection cycle

Task 1.9

The correct answer is: The ability to pay amounts when they are due

Task 1.10

The correct answer is: (i), (iv), (v) and (vi)

Bank references, credit agency references, trade references and recent financial statements would all be useful for assessing the credit status of a potential customer.

Task 1.11

The correct answer is: Purchase of a non-current asset in three equal instalments

Task 1.12

The correct answer is: Establishing customer credit status is part of the ordering cycle.

Task 1.13

The correct answer is: Net 30 days 2% discount for 10 days

Task 1.14

The correct answer is: (ii), (iii), (iv) and (vi)

Chapter 2

Task 2.1

The correct answer is: Aged receivables' analysis

This is used for an established customer not assessing a new customer.

Task 2.2

The correct answer is: Bank reference, Companies House, credit reference agency

Task 2.3

The correct answer is: All of the above

Task 2.4

Gross profit margin	25%
Operating profit margin	12%
Return on capital employed	10%
Net asset turnover	0.83 times

Workings:

(a) Gross profit margin = 125/500 × 100 = 25%
(b) Operating profit margin = 60/500 × 100 = 12%
(c) Return on capital employed = 60/600 × 100 = 10%
(d) Net asset turnover = 500/600 = 0.83 times

Task 2.5

Current ratio	1.9 : 1
Quick ratio	1.2 : 1
Inventory holding period	58 days
Accounts receivable collection period	58 days
Accounts payable payment period	73 days
Return on capital employed	5.4%
Gearing ratio	38%
Interest cover	1.75 times

Workings:

(a)   Current ratio = 210/108 = 1.9 : 1
(b)   Quick ratio = 130/108 = 1.2 : 1
(c)   Inventory holding period = (80/500) × 365 = 58 days
(d)   Accounts receivable collection period = (120/750) × 365 = 58 days
(e)   Accounts payable payment period = (100/500) × 365 = 73 days
(f)   Return on capital employed = ((250 − 180)/(802 + 500)) × 100 = 5.4%
(g)   Gearing ratio = (500/(802 + 500)) × 100 = 38%
(h)   Interest cover = (250 − 180)/40 = 1.75 times

Task 2.6

MEMO

To: Finance Director

From: Credit Controller

Date: X-X-20X8

Subject: Request for credit from Faverly Ltd

After the request from Faverly Ltd for £20,000 of credit I have examined the information that we have available about the company which includes a bank reference, two trade references and the financial statements for the last two years.

Bank reference

The bank reference is reasonable but not as positive as it might be.

Trade references

Both trade referees note that Faverly Ltd is an occasional late payer and one of the referees did in fact suspend credit with the company for six months in 20X6. It is interesting to note that both referees only allow Faverly Ltd credit of £10,000 on 30 days credit terms.

Financial statements

The financial statements for Faverly Ltd for the last two years have been examined and the following key ratios calculated under the headings of profitability, liquidity and gearing.

	20X8	20X7
Profitability		
Gross profit margin	22%	21%
Net profit margin	12.5%	12%
Return on capital employed	11.1%	10.5%
Liquidity		
Current ratio	0.54 : 1	0.67: 1
Quick ratio	0.3 : 1	0.4 : 1
Inventory holding period	52 days	45 days
Accounts receivable collection period	51 days	58 days
Accounts payable payment period	75 days	78 days
Gearing		
Interest cover	4.3 times	5.6 times

Although the company appears to be profitable and indeed to be increasing its profitability levels there has to be considerable concern about the company's liquidity. Both the current and quick ratios are seemingly very low and are decreasing. While the company has no long-term debt it has been financed for the last two years by a substantial overdraft although the interest cover is still quite healthy at over four times.

Concern should also be raised about the accounts payable payment period which although slightly improved is still long at 75 days and considerably longer than the company's accounts receivable collection period of 51 days.

Conclusion

In the absence of any further information I suggest that we offer Faverly Ltd a trial period of credit for £10,000 on strictly 30-day terms. If these terms are not adhered to strictly then we must trade on a cash basis only with the company.

Task 2.7

Finance director

Fisher Ltd

Date:

Dear Sir

Re: Request for credit facilities

Thank you for your enquiry regarding the provision of credit facilities of £15,000 on 30-day terms. We have taken up your trade references and examined your latest set of financial statements.

We are concerned about your levels of profitability, gearing and liquidity in the most recent year and also have some concerns about one of the trade references from Froggett & Sons.

On balance we are not in a position to grant your request for trade credit at the current time although we would, of course, be delighted to trade with you on a cash basis. If you do not wish to trade on this basis and would like to enquire about credit terms in the future then we would be delighted to examine your current year's financial statements when they are available and take up an alternative trade reference.

Thank you for your interest shown in our business.

Yours faithfully

Credit controller

Task 2.8

The correct answer is: (i), (iii) and (iv)

....

Task 2.9

The correct answer is: Statement (i) – False, Statement (ii) True

....

Task 2.10

To: Financial Controller

From: Assistant Accountant

Date: 17 January 20X8

Subject: Request for credit by Whittle Ltd

I have reviewed Whittle Ltd's financial statements and the references that we have received.

Ratio analysis

	This year	Last year
Current ratio	$\frac{1,090}{970} = 1.12$	$\frac{1,025}{958} = 1.07$
Acid test ratio	$\frac{890}{970} = 0.92$	$\frac{855}{958} = 0.89$
Gearing ratio	$\frac{500}{2,010} = 25\%$	$\frac{400}{1,517} = 26\%$

Current ratio

The current ratio is above 1, which means that **current assets** more than **cover current liabilities**. The current ratio has also risen since last year. The one reservation is that the rise has been due to an increase in inventory and receivables and cash has fallen slightly, indicating that control over working capital may be less efficient than in the previous year.

Quick ratio/Acid test ratio

As with the current ratio, the quick ratio has risen slightly during the year. Excluding inventory, **current assets nearly cover current liabilities** should these need to be paid.

Gearing ratio

Equity has remained at about three times long-term loan capital indicating that Whittle Ltd is **reasonably geared**. The gearing ratio has only fallen slightly this year despite extra borrowings (non-current liabilities) of £100,000, indicating that Whittle Ltd should be able to afford the extra debt.

References

The reference from **Greatlygrow Ltd** does not indicate any problems. However, Whittle Ltd has only been trading with Greatlygrow Ltd for one year, a reasonably successful one for Whittle Ltd.

Whittle Ltd has had a **much longer trading relationship**, five years, with **Weston Ltd**. However, the reference indicates that credit was suspended two years ago for six months. Despite the past problems Weston is giving Whittle Ltd two months' credit.

Recommendations

Before a final decision is taken about whether to grant credit to Whittle Ltd, **clarification of the reasons for the suspension of credit should be obtained**, and also whether there have been any other **breaches of credit terms**. A further reference, either from another long-term supplier or from Whittle Ltd's bank, needs to be obtained.

If the explanations and further reference is satisfactory, I recommend credit should be extended to Whittle Ltd. The credit period should initially be one month, and the account should be **closely monitored**. A **financial limit** should also be set; but you will want to consider the **size of the limit** and what should happen if the **value of the order exceeds** the desirable limit.

Task 2.11

(a)   To: Financial Controller

From: Accounting Technician

Date:

Subject: Request for credit facilities

We have received an application from David Jones, Financial Controller of Dreams Ltd, for credit of £20,000 on 60-day terms. However, I have the following reservations about this request.

- Dreams Ltd has **only supplied the statement of profit or loss**, not the Statement of Financial Position, restricting the financial analysis we can carry out.

- The financial statements are now **over six months old**.

- **Gross profit** and **gross profit margin** have **fallen slightly** between 20X7 and 20X8.

- The company made a **loss after tax** in 20X7 and only a small profit in 20X8.

- The terms given by the two suppliers who have provided references are stricter than the terms that Dreams Ltd has requested, £10,000 for 30 days in one case, £2,500 for 30 days in the other.

- Dreams Ltd has **not kept** to the **terms** set by Carpet Ltd, and has been taking on average 60 days to settle its account with Carpet Ltd.

- Wardrobes Ltd has **only traded** with Dreams Ltd for **three months**, and thus the assurance given by its reference is limited.

Appendix – Ratios

	20X8	20X7
Gross profit margin	$\frac{550}{1,800} \times 100\% = 30.6\%$	$\frac{560}{1,750} \times 100\% = 32.0\%$

(b)

Sleepy Ltd
Tregarn Trading Estate
Cardiff
CF1 3EW

Mr D. Jones
Finance Director
Dreams Ltd
17 High Street
Newport
South Wales

Date:

Dear Mr Jones

Request for credit facilities

Thank you for your application for opening credit facilities. We are pleased that you are interested in doing business with our company.

We have considered your application against our prescribed credit criteria. At present we do not feel able to offer you the facilities you request, but may be able to offer a facility of £10,000 credit on 30 days terms. In order to be able to decide whether to offer this facility, we shall need to see copies of your Statement of Financial Position from the year ended 30 June 20X8 and your most recent management accounts.

We look forward to hearing from you, and hope that we shall soon be trading with you.

Yours sincerely

Task 2.12

The correct answer is: Cash is going out of the business more quickly than it is coming in

If receivables are taking longer to pay money into the business than the business is taking to pay its payables then money is going out quicker than it is coming in.

Task 2.13

The correct answer is: (i) and (ii) only

Task 2.14

The correct answer is: Do you think this customer has a good reputation?

It would not be appropriate to ask another business to make such a judgement.

Task 2.15

The correct answer is: 16.0%

(£149,000/(£400,000 + £380,000 + £150,000)) × 100 = 16.0%

Task 2.16

The correct answer is: They are not audited.

Task 2.17

The correct answer is: The figure gives a closer approximation to cash flow.

Task 2.18

The correct answer is: Details of supplier references

Task 2.19

Sales representatives on client visits can be asked to:

1. Observe the premises to gain an impression of whether the business looks busy/well managed.

    By witnessing how active the business is, the representative is in a position to say whether business is quiet. This might indicate that less cash will be available to settle accounts with suppliers.

2. Take note of any internal notice boards or overheard comments that might indicate the business is having difficulties.

    Notices asking for volunteers to work overtime would indicate that business is booming and that cash is available to pay suppliers. Rumours of redundancies might be a clue to be vigilant if the account becomes overdue.

Task 2.20

(a) **Complete the table below by calculating the key indicators (to two decimal places) for 20X6 and 20X5 for Ultra Ltd, and rate the company using the credit rating scoring system.**

Ultra Ltd	20X6 Indicator	20X6 Rating	20X5 Rating	20X5 Indicator
Operating profit margin %	9.10	5	3.35	0
Interest cover	3.40	0	1.41	−10
Current ratio	2.63	10	0.78	−20
Gearing %	52.15	0	65.38	−20
Total credit rating		15		−50

(b) **Based on the results of your credit rating and using the table above, recommend whether the requested credit limit should be given to Ultra Ltd.**

Customer	Decision
Ultra Ltd	Request latest management accounts and defer decision

Chapter 3

Task 3.1

The correct answer is: Intention to create legal relations, consideration, agreement

Task 3.2

The correct answer is: Offer

Task 3.3

The correct answer is: (i), (iii) and (iv)

Task 3.4

The correct answer is: Condition

Task 3.5

The correct answer is: Action for the price

Task 3.6

The correct answer is: County Court

Task 3.7

The correct answer is: A court bailiff seizes and sells the receivable's goods on behalf of the business.

Task 3.8

The correct answer is: A demand for payment from an outstanding receivable of £5,000 or more

Task 3.9

The correct answer is: Secured creditors, bankruptcy costs, preferential creditors, unsecured creditors

Task 3.10

The correct answer is: Unsecured creditors

Task 3.11

The correct answer is: Bankruptcy

Bankruptcy relates to individuals, not to companies.

Task 3.12

The correct answer is: An individual whose data is held

Task 3.13

The correct answer is: They do what they are expected to do.

Task 3.14

The correct answer is: Gross Debt × (base rate + 8%) × (No. of days overdue/365)

Task 3.15

The correct answer is: Slow track

Task 3.16

The correct answer is: Neither (i) nor (ii)

Task 3.17

The correct answer is: (ii) only

Consideration need only be sufficient – it need not be adequate.

Task 3.18

The correct answer is: An auction bid

The others are invitations to treat.

Task 3.19

The correct answer is: (i), (ii) and (iv)

Offer and acceptance, consideration and intention to create legal relations are essential requirements of a contract.

Task 3.20

The correct answer is: Express terms

Task 3.21

The correct answer is: 8

Task 3.22

The correct answer is: No. Brian's letter has varied the terms and so is a counter-offer, rejecting Alexander's original offer.

Brian varied the terms of the offer when replying to Alexander.

Task 3.23

The correct answer is: (ii) only

Task 3.24

The correct answer is: The promise of an exchange of value

Task 3.25

The contract between Karen and the sports retailer is voidable due to:

	✓
Unfair Contract	
Fraud	
Misrepresentation	✓
Consumer Credit	

Task 3.26

What is the amount of interest that Alex may charge Will under the Late Payment of Commercial Debts (Interest) Act? Calculate your answer to the nearest penny.

£ | 628.77

Task 3.27

Identify whether the following statements about the Data Protection Act are true or false.

	True ✓	False ✓
Data cannot be kept for more than six months.		✓
Individuals have a right to object to decisions taken where there is no human involvement.	✓	
An internet company that wishes to use data collected from individuals for marketing purposes must have the permission of those individuals.	✓	
Information gathered by using CCTV security cameras is not subject to the Data Protection Act rules.		✓

Task 3.28

Drag and drop the correct words into the following statement.

A retention of title clause within a contract is [expressly stated] . It allows the

supplier to [retain] ownership of the goods supplied. An official receiver

[does not have to] seek the authority of an insolvency practitioner before

deciding that a claim is valid. If an official receiver sells goods that are subject to
a valid retention of title claim by the supplier he or she [can be] liable to
pay damages to the supplier.

∙∙

Task 3.29

**Creditors have several options to enforce a county court judgement.
Match each option to the explanation by clicking on the left box first
then on the corresponding right box. You can remove a line by
clicking on it.**

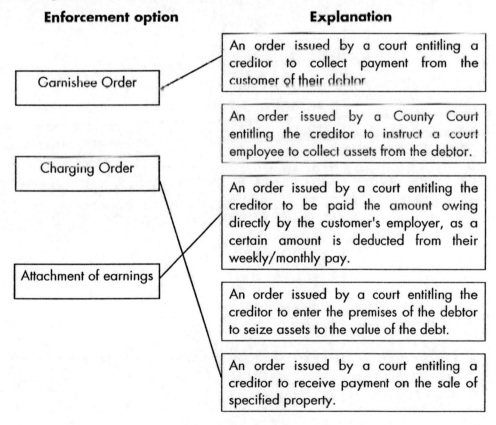

Enforcement option

Garnishee Order

Charging Order

Attachment of earnings

Explanation

An order issued by a court entitling a creditor to collect payment from the customer of their debtor

An order issued by a County Court entitling the creditor to instruct a court employee to collect assets from the debtor.

An order issued by a court entitling the creditor to be paid the amount owing directly by the customer's employer, as a certain amount is deducted from their weekly/monthly pay.

An order issued by a court entitling the creditor to enter the premises of the debtor to seize assets to the value of the debt.

An order issued by a court entitling a creditor to receive payment on the sale of specified property.

Chapter 4

Task 4.1

The correct answer is: 7.4%

$$\text{Cost of discount} = \frac{d}{100-d} \times \frac{365}{N-D}$$

where d = discount percentage given

N = normal payment term

D = discount payment term

$$\text{Cost of discount} \quad \frac{1}{100-1} \times \frac{365}{60-10} = 7.4\%$$

Task 4.2

The correct answer is: Cost = 18.8%, Introduce or not = No.

$$\text{Cost of early settlement} = \frac{d}{(100-d)} \times \frac{365}{(N-D)}$$

$$= \frac{3}{(100-3)} \times \frac{365}{(60-0)}$$

$$= 18.8\%$$

As 18.8% is greater than the 15% the company uses to appraise investments, the discount is not worthwhile.

Task 4.3

The correct answer is: 17.7%

$$\text{Cost of discount} = \left(\frac{d}{100-d} \times \frac{365}{(N-D)} \right)\%$$

$$= \left(\frac{2.5}{100-2.5} \times \frac{365}{60-7} \right)\%$$

$$= 17.7\%$$

Task 4.4

The correct answer is: £240,000

The existing value of receivables is: $\dfrac{\text{£18m}}{12\,\text{months}} = \text{£1.5m}$

If sales increased by 60,000 units, the value of receivables would be:

$$2 \times \dfrac{\text{£18m} + (60,000 \times \text{£10})}{12\,\text{months}} = \text{£3.1 million}$$

The receivables have to be financed somehow, and the additional £1.6 million will cost £1,600,000 × 15% = £240,000 in financing costs.

Task 4.5

The correct answer is: Despatch of goods

Task 4.6

The correct answer is: (ii) only

The amounts advanced by the invoice discounter are at a discount to the carrying amount (book value) of the receivables.

Task 4.7

The correct answer is: A business lends money to a customer based on a discounted value of the invoices that customer has issued

Task 4.8

The correct answer is: Claim back amounts owed to it by customers who have defaulted

Task 4.9

The correct answer is: Whole turnover policy

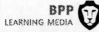

Task 4.10

The correct answer is: Statement (i) and statement (ii) are both false.

Statement (i) describes a credit reference agency. Statement (ii) describes the services of a factor. A credit collection agency specialises in the collection of debts that are proving difficult to obtain in the normal course of business.

Task 4.11

The correct answer is: Neither statement is true

Task 4.12

The correct answer is:

$$\text{Cost of discount} \quad = \quad \frac{1.5}{100-1.5} \times \frac{365}{30-14} \times 100$$

$$= \quad 34.7\%$$

Not worthwhile as the cost of bank interest is only 6%.

Task 4.13

The correct answer is: A percentage of amounts collected

Task 4.14

The correct answer is: (ii), (iii) and (v)

Overdraft interest should be saved as the money is received from the factor earlier than the receivables would have paid. As the money is received earlier, it should be possible to pay suppliers earlier, avoiding interest from suppliers or late payment penalties.

Task 4.15

The correct answer is: Re-instigating receivables ledger

Task 4.16

The correct answer is: About 80% of receivables are covered for their entire amount.

Task 4.17

The correct answer is: £50,000 increase

Working:

New receivables	=	£390,000 × 2/12
	=	£65,000
Current receivables	=	£25,000
Increase in receivables	=	£40,000
Increase in cash due to extra revenue	=	£390,000 – £300,000
	=	£90,000
Increase in cash	=	£90,000 – £40,000
	=	£50,000

Task 4.18

The correct answer is: 27.34%

Working:

Cost of discount	=	3/97 = 0.0309278 + 1 = 1.0309278
	=	365/(60–14) = 7.9347826
	=	$1.0309278^{7.9347826}$
	=	1.27339545547
	=	1.27339545547 – 1
	=	0.27339545547 × 100
	=	27.34%

Task 4.19

The correct answer is: (ii), (iv) and (v)

Task 4.20

The correct answer is: (i) only

Task 4.21

SNN is offering   a recourse factoring facility   .

KWN can borrow: £   2,100,000

Task 4.22

Email

To: Sales Staff   **Date:**   Today

From: AAT Technician   **Subject:**   Early Settlement Discounts

Please find below my explanation of how an annual percentage cost of an early settlement discount is calculated.

The effective rate of interest

If a customer pays promptly to take advantage of a 3% early settlement discount, we will receive 97% of the invoice total. This means that the discount we are giving the customer is   3.09   of the amount they pay us. This is what it costs us to receive the cash earlier than our normal credit terms. It is called the effective rate of interest.

Discount periods

If the normal credit terms require customers to pay within 30 days of receiving an invoice, and the discount applies if the customer pays within 14 days, we are offering the discount in return for paying 16 days earlier than our normal terms. There are   22.81   discount periods of 16 days in a 365 day year.

Annual percentage cost of the early settlement discount using simple interest rates

The annual percentage cost is found   multiplying   by the effective rate of interest and the discount periods in a year. The annual percentage cost of offering 2% discount to customers paying within 14 days rather than 30 days is   70   to the nearest whole percent. I trust this will help you in any discussions with customers about early settlement discounts.

AAT Technician

Chapter 5

Task 5.1

The correct answer is: The maximum amount allowed to be outstanding at any point in time

Task 5.2

	Total £	Credit limit £	Current, < 30 days £	31–60 days £	61–90 days £	> 90 days £
Knightly Ltd	24,519	30,000	11,333	8,448	4,738	

Task 5.3

Jeremy Ltd – There is one long-outstanding amount of £890 which would appear to be a problem. The customer's file should be checked to see if there is any correspondence about this amount and if not a telephone call should be made to the customer to determine the problem with the payment. Consideration might be given to providing an allowance for this amount as a doubtful debt.

Lenter Ltd – This receivable would appear to be a consistent slow payer as the amounts are equally stretched over the current period up to 90 days. The customer should be consulted about its slow payment record and incentives for earlier payment such as settlement discounts offered.

Friday Partners – This amount is of great concern as not only has it been outstanding for more than 61 days but there is no current trading with the customer. The customer should be contacted urgently in order to determine any problem with the payment of the debt.

Diamond & Co – This customer appears to be a slightly slow payer but of more importance is that their credit limit has been exceeded by over £1,000. The reason for this exceeding of the credit limit should be investigated and if necessary no further sales to this customer should be made until the earlier invoices are paid.

Task 5.4

MEMORANDUM

To: Sales Manager

From: Credit Controller

Date: 6 December

Subject: Aged receivables' analysis

Megacorp plc

32% of this major customer's debt is over 90 days old. Although clearly a key customer, Megacorp plc appears to be taking unfair advantage of its 60 days net credit terms.

For the future, we should consider:

(a)   Offering a discount for early payment

(b)   Improving communication with Megacorp plc's payables ledger department and senior management to help ensure prompt payment

(c)   Sending prompt reminder letters, followed up by telephone calls

(d)   Reviewing the credit limit for the company

Goodfellows Cycles Ltd

Goodfellows Cycles Ltd appears generally to be a prompt payer within the 30 days terms set for the customer. However, a debt of £5,000 is currently outstanding for over 90 days.

I recommend that:

(a)   The £5,000 debt outstanding for over 90 days should be investigated to check whether there is some dispute. Perhaps a relatively minor query is holding up payment.

(b)   We should consider ways of increasing sales to the customer.

(c)   Procedures for dealing with customer queries should be reviewed.

Hooper-bikes Ltd

Hooper-bikes has a total amount outstanding in excess of its credit limit. 60 days' credit is allowed to this customer, but 40% of its debt is overdue. This is not a satisfactory situation, and urgent action should be taken.

For the future, I recommend that:

(a)   The credit limit for the customer should be reviewed

(b)   We make sure that the debt outstanding is brought to within the current credit limit as soon as possible

(c) We consider how to improve this customer's payment record, perhaps by insisting on cash with order

(d) We review order procedures to avoid customers being supplied with goods which take their account beyond its credit limit

Dynamo Cycles Ltd

There are no current problems regarding this smaller customer's account. Credit taken up is within the credit limit and no debt is overdue.

For the future we might:

(a) Try to increase sales to Dynamo
(b) Review this customer's credit limit

Task 5.5

Carnford Ltd – The amount is more than 60 days overdue and a visit to the customer might be in order to see if we can obtain payment without resort to legal proceedings. If a visit is not successful then legal proceedings should be considered subject to the agreement of the finance director. As the amount is large and over 60 days overdue, an allowance should be made for the entire amount.

Luxford Ltd – A telephone call should be made to remind the company that there is a balance of £900 overdue and, in particular, to discover the reason for the amount of £180 that has been overdue for more than 60 days. No allowance is necessary as yet.

KLP Ltd – All of the amount outstanding is overdue and £960 is at least 30 days overdue. The customer should be considered being placed on the stop list and a meeting arranged to clarify the position.

Flanders Ltd – This appears to be a consistent customer but of the total overdue amount of £8,210, £1,985 is more than 30 days overdue. A reminder letter and telephone call should be made to the customer and consideration should be given to putting the customer on the stop list. However, as this seems to be a regular customer this should only be done after serious consideration especially if other negotiations will suffice.

Task 5.6

Finance Controller

Harvey Ltd

Date:

Dear Sir

Account No: 204764

I do not appear to have received payment of the amount of £1,350.46 which is 14 days overdue. I trust that this is an oversight and that you will arrange for immediate payment to be made. If you are withholding payment for any reason, please contact me urgently and I will be pleased to assist you.

If you have already made payment please advise me and accept my apology for having troubled you.

Yours faithfully

Credit Controller

....

Task 5.7

Financial Controller

Bart & Sons

Date:

Dear Sir

Account No: B245

I do not appear to have received payment of the amount of £976.80 which is now 30 days overdue. I trust that this is an oversight and that you will arrange for immediate payment to be made. If you are withholding payment for any reason, please contact me urgently and I will be pleased to assist you.

I regret that unless payment is received within the next seven days I will have no alternative but to stop any further sales on credit to you until the amount owing is cleared in full. If you have already made payment please advise me and accept my apology for having troubled you.

Yours faithfully

Credit Controller

....

Task 5.8

The correct answer is: If 20% of the largest customers are analysed this should account for 80% in value.

....

Task 5.9

Manton Ltd Aged Receivables' Analysis – 31 October 20X7

Customer name and ref	Total amount	Current < 1 month	Outstanding 1-2 months	Outstanding 2-3 months	Outstanding > 3 months
New Milton	£13,000	£4,000 M98	£2,000 M89		£7,000 M17
Sway	£1,000		£1,000 M81		
Mudeford	£0				
Barton	£17,000	£4,000 M101		£13,000 M69	
Boscombe	£5,000	£5,000 M103			
TOTAL	£36,000	£13,000	£3,000	£13,000	£7,000

Task 5.10

The correct answer is: Largest debts should be pursued as a first priority with smallest amounts pursued last.

Task 5.11

The correct answer is: Telephone Jines Ltd to enquire about the situation in order to determine whether there is any query regarding the amount outstanding and to agree steps for payment.

Task 5.12

The correct answer is: £4,277

These are the April and May outstanding amounts.

Task 5.13

The correct answer is: An irrecoverable debt is written off and does not appear in the statement of financial position.

Task 5.14

The correct answer is: Inventory ordering

Inventory ordering would not be part of an organisation's credit control policy.

Task 5.15

The correct answer is: (i), (ii) and (v)

Task 5.16

The correct answer is: At any point in time the customer's balance must not exceed £10,000.

Task 5.17

The correct answer is: It could result in an irrecoverable debt.

Task 5.18

The correct answer is: £3,119

£1,890 + £1,560 – £331

Task 5.19

The correct answer is: 80/20 rule

Task 5.20

The correct answer is: Neither statement

A doubtful debt may not be received but an allowance is made against it rather than removing it from the statement of financial position.

Task 5.21

The correct answer is: (i) and (iii)

Task 5.22

The correct answer is: Discuss the situation with the customer

Task 5.23

The correct answer is: £2,610

Task 5.24

The correct answer is: Customer in liquidation

Task 5.25

The correct answer is: An amount owing from a customer who has not answered the telephone, replied to letters and is no longer at their trading address

If there are discussions or legal proceedings including administration then there is a likelihood of the debt being recovered. However, if the customer no longer appears to exist then this is more than likely to be an irrecoverable debt.

Task 5.26

Which of the following conditions must have been met for a business to successfully claim VAT Bad Debt Relief from HMRC?

	✓
The customer must have ceased trading and not paid one or more invoices due to the business.	
Ownership of the items invoiced must have been transferred to the customer.	
The business making the claim must have written the debt off as bad (irrecoverable).	✓
The debt must be at least 12 months old.	

Task 5.27

Calculate the amount that Scott should write off as an irrecoverable debt. Ignore VAT. Show your answer to the nearest penny.

£	10,237.50

Task 5.28

It is of the utmost importance that Conic acts with urgency on this matter as the receiver has only just been appointed.

- Speed is of the essence in case the receiver uses the goods in any way.

- Conic does have a standard ROT clause, so a visit to the premises of Lomond is worthwhile.

- If this is some distance away, it may be possible to appoint an agent to visit on Conic's behalf.

- If the ROT clause turns out to be unsuccessful, Lomond will fail to be an unsecured creditor of Conic and will be unlikely to receive much, if any of the outstanding debt.

- The total invoice value is for £140,000 (£20,000 + £120,000).

- The account is credit insured for 80% of the debt, therefore a claim should be made to the insurer for £96,000 ((80% × £20,000 = £16,000) + (80% × (£120,000/1.2) = £80,000)).

- A provision should be made for the balance of £24,000 (£120,000 – £96,000).

- There will be no claim for HMRC bad debt relief on the invoice for the nutritional products (£20,000) as VAT on this will be zero (foodstuff) however VAT of £20,000 can be reclaimed on sportswear after six months and after the debt has been written off.

Task 5.29

Connoly seem to have used a variety of excuse and delaying tactics, while Pyllon has done its best to prove the amount owed. The debt is now substantially overdue (payment was due by 31 March, it is now 30 June, so the debt is 90 days old) with no apparent reason, even though Connoly are normally slow payers.

A credit control policy is in place to ensure that Pyllon does not suffer any unnecessary liquidity problems or unnecessary bad debts. Because there is no business reason for not pursuing the debt in accordance with the credit control policy, Pyllon should proceed to instruct a debt collection agency or commence legal action.

Causing 'unplesantness' is not a sufficient reason for Pyllon not to protect its business position. The HR director's personal situation should have no bearing on Pyllon's business decisions and she should not use her position as a director to influence how a policy should be applied for her own personal gain.

AAT AQ2016 SAMPLE ASSESSMENT 1 CREDIT MANAGEMENT

Time allowed: 2 hours and 30 minutes

Credit Management (CDMT)
AAT sample assessment 1

Task 1 (18 marks)

(a) **Drag and drop the correct words into the following statement.**

Terms specifically stated in a contract are known as [　　　　] terms, which are [　　　　] for both parties. Terms that are fundamental to a contract are known as [　　　　]. If they are broken, the party breaking them will be in breach or contract and can be sued for [　　　　].

The drag and drop choices are:

binding
conditions
damages
express
guarantees
optional
termination
warranties

Gustav owes Holst £25,000 excluding VAT, which is charged at the standard rate. The debt has been overdue for 90 days. The current Bank of England base rate is 0.5%.

(b) **What is the amount of interest that Holst may charge Gustav under the Late Payment of Commercial Debts (Interest) Act? Calculate your answer to the nearest penny.**

£ [　　　　]

(c) **Identify whether the following statements about the Data Protection Act are true or false.**

	True ✓	False ✓
Companies are able to find out what information is held about them on computer-based records.		
Individuals have a right to object to decisions taken where there is no human involvement.		
Individuals cannot request that data relating to them will not be used for direct marketing purposes.		
Data cannot be kept for more than six months.		

Sanjay orders 500 sweaters from an online fashion supplier. The sweaters are described as 100% wool. When the sweaters arrive, Sanjay checks the labels and sees that the material is described as 50% wool, 50% man-made fibres.

(d) **The contract between Sanjay and the fashion supplier is voidable due to:**

	✓
Unfair Contract	
Fraud	
Misrepresentation	
Consumer Credit	

(e) **Identify whether the following statements about consideration in contract law are true or false.**

Consideration has to be in the form of goods or money.	▼
Consideration can be in the form of agreeing to perform an existing public duty.	▼
Consideration can be a promise to do something in the future.	▼

Drop-down list:

True
False

Task 2 (24 marks)

Floortiles Ltd uses a credit rating system to assess the credit status of new customers. The credit rating (scoring) system below is used to assess the risk of default by calculating key indicators (ratios), comparing them to the table and calculating an aggregate score.

Credit rating (scoring) system Operating profit margin	Score
Losses	–5
Less than 5%	0
5% and above but less than 10%	5
10% and above but less than 20%	10
20% or more	20
Interest cover	
No cover	–30
Less than 1	–20
1 and above but less than 2	–10
2 and above but less than 4	0
4 or more	10

Credit rating (scoring) system Current ratio	Score
Less than 1	–20
1 and above but less than 1.25	–10
1.25 and above but less than 1.5	0
1.5 or more	10
Gearing (total debt/total debt plus equity)	
Less than 25%	20
25% and above but less than 50%	10
50% and above but less than 65%	0
65% and above but less than 75%	–20
75% and above but less than 80%	–40
80% or more	–100

Risk	Aggregate score
Very low risk	Between 60 and 21
Low risk	Between 20 and 1
Medium risk	Between 0 and –24
High risk	Between –25 and –50
Very high risk	Between –51 and –160

The sales department has asked for a credit limit of £45,000 to be given to Bathrooms Ltd, a potential new customer. The financial information below has been supplied by Bathrooms Ltd.

Bathrooms Ltd Statement of Profit or Loss

	20X5 £000	20X4 £000
Sales revenue	9,870	8,624
Cost of sales	7,405	6,900
Gross profit	**2,465**	**1,724**
Distribution costs	982	850
Administration expenses	1,000	1,000
Operating profit/(loss)	**483**	**(126)**
Finance costs	200	105
Profit/(loss) before taxation	**283**	**(231)**
Taxation	60	0
Profit/(loss) for the year	**223**	**(231)**

Bathrooms Ltd Statement of Financial Position

	20X5 £000	20X4 £000
Assets		
Non-current assets		
Property, plant and equipment	3,869	2,700
Current assets		
Inventories	364	350
Trade and other receivables	192	177
Cash	5	9
	561	536
Total assets	**4,430**	**3,236**

	20X5 £000	20X4 £000
Equity and liabilities		
Equity		
Share capital	1,500	1,500
Retained earnings	464	241
Total Equity	**1,964**	**1,741**
Non-current liabilities		
Borrowing	2,000	1,050
Current liabilities		
Borrowing	110	0
Trade and other payables	356	445
Total liabilities	**2,466**	**1,495**
Total equity and liabilities	**4,430**	**3,326**

(a) **Complete the table below by calculating the key indicators (to two decimal places) for 20X5 and 20X4 for Bathrooms Ltd, and rate the company using the credit rating scoring system.**

Bathrooms Ltd	20X5 Indicator	20X5 Rating	20X4 Indicator	20X4 Rating
Operating profit margin %				
Interest cover				
Current ratio				
Gearing %				
Total credit rating				

Rating	Decision
Very low or low risk current year and very low or low risk previous year	Accept
Very low or low risk current year and medium risk previous year	Accept
Very low or low risk current year and high or very high risk previous year	Request latest management accounts and defer decision
Very high risk or high risk current year	Reject
Medium risk current year and medium, low or very low risk previous year	Accept
Medium risk current year and high or very high risk previous year	Request latest management accounts and defer decision

(b) **Based on the results of your credit rating and using the table above, recommend whether the requested credit limit should be given to Bathrooms Ltd.**

Customer	Decision	
Bathrooms Ltd		▼

Drop-down list:

Accept
Reject
Request latest management accounts and defer decision

Task 3 (30 marks)

Berlin Ltd is a potential new customer and has approached Milan Ltd to ask for a credit limit of £50,000.

Milan Ltd has standard terms of trade of 30 days.

The sales director has advised you that she has invited the directors of Berlin Ltd to play golf next month, as she is keen to gain Berlin's business. The sales director receives a bonus based on the amount of new business she brings in.

(a) **Write notes to brief a new member of the credit control team explaining three sources of external information you will use (other than financial statements) when assessing whether to grant credit to a new customer. Comment on the role of the sales director in the credit assessment process.**

Berlin has supplied the following information based on the last two years of trading.

Berlin Limited statement of financial position

	20X5 £000	20X4 £000
ASSETS		
Non-current assets		
Property, plant and equipment	8,399	15,473
Current assets		
Inventories	858	1,145
Trade and other receivables	2,407	2,655
Cash	5	5
	3,270	**3,805**
Total assets	**11,669**	**19,278**

	20X5 £000	20X4 £000
EQUITY AND LIABILITIES		
Equity		
Share capital	2,500	2,500
Retained earnings	2,324	1,135
Total Equity	**4,824**	**3,635**
Non-current liabilities		
Borrowing	3,825	10,200
Current liabilities		
Trade and other payables	2,144	2,671
Taxation	376	272
Borrowing	500	2,500
	3,020	**5,443**
Total liabilities	**6,845**	**15,643**
Total equity and liabilities	**11,669**	**19,278**

Berlin Limited statement of profit or loss

	20X5 £000	20X4 £000
Sales revenue	28,340	29,380
Cost of sales	22,360	23,210
Gross profit	**5,980**	**6,170**
Distribution costs	2,580	2,100
Administration expenses	1,350	1,250
Operating profit	**2,050**	**2,820**
Finance costs	485	1,525
Profit before taxation	**1,565**	**1,295**
Taxation	376	272
Profit for the year	**1,189**	**1,023**

Berlin Limited

	20X5	20X4
Gross profit margin %	21.1	21.0
Operating profit margin %	7.23	9.60
Interest cover	4.23	1.85
Current ratio	1.08	0.70
Trade payables payment period in days	35.0	42.0
Trade receivables collection period in days	31.0	32.98
Inventory holding period in days	14.01	18.01
Gearing %	47.27	77.75

The following additional information has also been provided.

1.   Berlin Ltd sells catering supplies. but also hires out larger equipment and machinery. Up to 20X4, much of Berlin's plant and equipment was acquired by means of finance leases. From 20X5 onwards, most of the equipment is acquired by using operating leases.

2.   Non-current assets acquired under finance leases are shown in the statement of financial position with the corresponding liability shown as part of borrowing.

3.   Interest charges on the finance leases are included as part of the finance costs in the income statement.

4.   Non-current assets acquired under operating leases are not shown in the statement of financial position. Payments relating to operating leases are included in the cost of sales. Commitments under operating leases are disclosed by way of a note. The operating lease note to the financial statements is shown below.

Operating lease note

	20X5 £000	20X5 £000
Annual commitments under non-cancellable operating leases which expire:		
within one year	2,110	200
in the second to fifth year inclusive	9,350	800
over five years	430	0

(b)   Write a note analysing the information and recommending whether credit should be granted.

Task 4 (20 marks)

The sales department of Rosemary Limited has asked for a credit limit of £55,000 to be given to Thyme Limited who is a potential new customer. The financial information below has been supplied by Thyme Limited in respect of the last two years. Rosemary Ltd trades on 30-day terms.

Thyme Limited statement of profit of loss

	20X5	20X4
Sales revenue	17,500	12,400
Cost of sales	12,450	7,875
Gross profit	**5,050**	**4,525**
Distribution costs	1,150	1,105
Administration expenses	1,541	1,655
Operating profit	**2,359**	**1,765**
Finance costs	390	280
Profit before taxation	**1,969**	**1,485**
Taxation	395	300
Profit for the year	**1,574**	**1,185**

Thyme Limited statement of financial position

	20X5 £000	20X4 £000
Assets		
Non-current assets		
Property, plant and equipment	6,996	6,313
Current assets		
Inventories	2,608	1,295
Trade and other receivables	3,803	1,992
Cash	0	5
	6,411	**3,292**
Total assets	**13,407**	**9,605**
Equity and liabilities		
Equity		
Share capital	3,500	3,500
Retained earnings	2,889	1,520
Total Equity	**6,389**	**5,020**
Non-current liabilities		
Borrowing	2,500	2,500
Current liabilities		
Bank overdraft	1,200	200
Trade and other payables	3,318	1,885
Total liabilities	**7,018**	**4,585**
Total equity and liabilities	**13,407**	**9,605**

Complete the email to the chief credit controller, calculating and commenting on key ratios, and conclude by recommending whether or not credit should be extended. All calculations should be given to two decimal in places.

Email

To: Credit Controller   **Date:** Today

From: AAT Technician   **Subject:** New Customer
Thyme Ltd

Please find below my calculations, observations and recommendation for new customer Thyme Ltd.

Profitability

Turnover has increased by (1) [▾] . Gross profit margin in 20X4 was [ ] % and [ ] % in 20X5.

Operating profit itself has increased by (2) [▾] , however the operating profit margin in 20X5 was [ ] % as compared to [ ] % in 20X4. This means that (3) [▾] although there might be some signs of possible (4) [▾] which need to be investigated further.

Interest can be covered (5) [▾] in both years.

Drop-down lists:

(1)   29.14%
       58.1%
       41.13%

(2)   33.65%
       25.18%
       74.82

(3)   the cost of sales has been well controlled
       expenses have been well controlled
       sales have been well controlled

(4)   overtrading
        undertrading
        over capitalisation
        under capitalisation

(5)   almost 16 times
        over 6 times
        over 4 times

Liquidity

Both the current ratio and the quick (acid test) ratio have (1) [▼] . In order to understand the liquidity position further it is important to review the trade cycles and the individual components making up the ratios.

Inventory has increased by [ ] %. When compared to the increase in turnover this might indicate that Thyme is planning further increases in sales. The inventory holding period has increased from [ ] days in 20X4 to [ ] days in 20X5.

This means that (2) [▼]

The trade receivables collection period has (3) [▼] . Trade receivables have increased by (4) [▼] .

This might mean that (5) [▼] .

The payables payment period is (6) [▼] our standard terms of trade.

The company has no cash in 20X5 and is more reliant on (7) [▼] .

Drop-down lists:

(1)   improved
        deteriorated

(2)   Thyme may run out of inventory
        funds are tied up in inventory
        suppliers are happy to extend credit

(3)   improved by over 20 days
        worsened by over 20 days

(4)   90.91%
        47.62%
        95.04%

(5)   Thyme has an effective credit control department
        Thyme is offering more generous terms to encourage sales

(6)   slightly less than
        slightly more than
        significantly more than
        significantly less than

(7)   short-term borrowing
        long-term borrowing

Recommendation

I recommend that [▼]

Drop-down lists:

we offer the credit as requested.
we refuse any credit.
we offer a lower credit limit for a trial period and request further information.

Task 5 (22 marks)

(a)   **Match each type or claim on the left to the appropriate type of court procedure on the right.** *(CBT instruction: Click on the left box first then on the corresponding right box. You can remove a line by clicking on it.)*

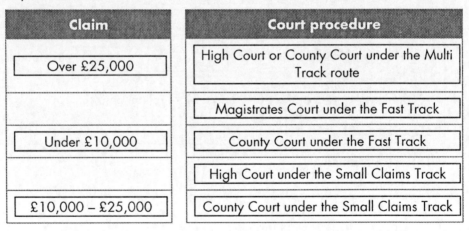

Claim	Court procedure
	High Court or County Court under the Multi Track route
Over £25,000	
	Magistrates Court under the Fast Track
Under £10,000	County Court under the Fast Track
	High Court under the Small Claims Track
£10,000 – £25,000	County Court under the Small Claims Track

(b) **Which of the following statements are true If a retention of title claim is to be successfully enforced?**

	True	False
The goods subject to the clause must be clearly identifiable.		
Goods which have been altered cannot usually be repossessed.		
The goods subject to the clause must be in the customer's warehouse.		
There must be a rentention of title clause shown on every invoice sent to the customer.		

XYZ Ltd is considering alternative ways of managing debt collection. XYZ's total receivables ledger balance as at 30 June 20X5 is £2,560,000, which includes £180,000 of debts that are over 90 days.

ABC Co. can provide XYZ with a facility whereby ABC manages the receivables ledger on behalf of XYZ. ABC will lend XYZ a maximum of £1,750,000, or 75% of the outstanding receivables balance, excluding debts over 90 days. ABC will not provide any protection against irrecoverable debts.

(c) **Complete the following sentences.**

ABC is offering [_____ ▼].

XYZ can borrow: [£ [_____]]

Drop-down list:

a non-recourse factoring facility
a recourse factoring facility
a non-recourse invoice discounting facility
a recourse invoice discounting facility

(d) **Which of the following are stages in a company winding up procedure?**

(i)   Statutory demand
(ii)   Petition to the Court
(iii) Bankruptcy order
(iii) Appointment or Administrator

	✓
(i), (ii) and (iii)	
(i) and (ii)	
All of the above	
(ii) and (iv)	

(e) **Drag and drop the correct words into the following statement.**

An aged receivables analysis is a management tool that can be used to highlight customers who are ⬚ .

It analyses the balance due from each customer according to the ⬚ of each invoice outstanding.

Analysis of trade receivables can also be undertaken based on focusing attention on ⬚ of customer accounts which make up ⬚ of the total value of outstanding debts.

The drag and drop choices are:

amount
80%
a bad credit risk
20%
slow to pay
50%
date
100%

Christopher owes Jayne £7,500 for goods supplied.

(f) **What is the normal remedy for Jayne as a result of non payment of the debt?**

	✓
Action for breach	
Action for price	
Specific injunction	
Action for restitution	

Task 6 (16 marks)

DEF Ltd wishes to claim VAT bad debt relief on some unpaid customer invoices.

(a)   Identify whether each statement below is true or false.

In order for DEF Ltd to be able to successfully reclaim VAT on an unpaid debt:

	True or False
DEF Ltd must have already accounted for the VAT and paid it over to HMRC	▼
The claim must be made within three years of the due date of payment of the debt	▼
DEF Ltd must have made a provision for the unpaid debt	▼
The debt must have remained unpaid for six months after the due date of payment	▼

Drop-down list:

True
False

Meerkat Ltd wishes to offer a 2% discount to its customers for settlement of invoices within 21 days. Meerkat's standard terms of trade are 45 days.

(b)   Calculate the following to two decimal places:

The simple annual cost of the discount ☐ %

The compound annual cost of the discount ☐ %

(c)   Which ONE of the following is an important aspect of liquidity management?

	✓
Having enough assets to meet all obligations on a timely basis	
Being able to pay all suppliers and other operational costs as they fall due	
Being profitable enough to settle amounts due when they become payable	
Rescheduling loan repayments to ensure they are non-current liabilities	

Jonty's customers currently pay 30 days after the month end. He is introducing a 1% discount from month 2 if customers settle the invoice in the same month. It is expected that 80% of customers will take advantage of this. The expected sales revenue per month is as follows:

	Sales revenue £
Month 1	95,000
Month 2	105,000
Month 3	136,000

(d) Expected cash receipts in month 3 will be:

£ [   ]

(e) Which ONE or the following is NOT a type of credit insurance?

	✓
Key account	
Catastrophe	
Unlimited excess	
Whole turnover	

Tom has received a letter from the liquidator of Jerry Ltd. The liquidator has indicated that all unsecured creditors of Jerry will receive a dividend of 2.5p in the pound (£) later in the year. Tom is owed £7,500 by Jerry.

(f) Calculate the amount that Tom should write off as an irrecoverable debt. Ignore VAT. Show your answer to the nearest penny.

£ [   ]

* *

Task 7 (20 marks)

Softfruit Ltd manufactures and supplies computer components. It also assembles and supplies computers made to individual customer specifications. VAT is charged at the standard rate on all supplies.

Softfruit includes an all monies retention of title clause as part of its standard terms of trade. Computers that are custom made to a specific customer order carry a unique serial number for warranty purposes. Payment terms are 30 days from the invoice date.

Softfruit has credit insurance for certain named customer accounts.

You work in the credit control department of Softfruit. Your supervisor is away on holiday and is not contactable, however you have been provided with the information below. Today's date is 30 June.

(a) **Review the information provided for each customer below and prepare comments and an action plan for dealing with the outstanding amounts due to Softfruit. Your action plan should include a summary of the options available to Softfruit to pursue outstanding amounts, along with recommendations for provisions or write off of irrecoverable debts where appropriate.**

FDP

FDP is a regular customer of Softfruit and always pays to terms. FDP is responsible for 15% of Softfruits annual turnover. FDP had ordered 12 custom-built computers for use in a new software development project. The order had specified that all 12 computers were to be delivered by 16 April in time for the project to begin. Softfruit delivered six computers on 15 April. However, due to the extended illness of their computer engineer Softfruit could only deliver the remaining six computers on 25 April.

The total value of the invoice to FDP dated 25 April is £72,000 including VAT. FDP has complained about the late delivery, stating that this has significantly delayed their important project. They are withholding payment and asking for compensation.

Gigabits

Softfruit has received notification that Gigabits is in receivership. The amount of the outstanding debt is £28,620 including VAT. The receiver has told Softfruit that she will not accept any retention of title claim as the goods in question are generic computer components that Gigabits has purchased from a number of suppliers. It will therefore not be possible to identify which had been supplied by Softfruit.

The account is credit insured for a maximum of 75% of the net debt or £15,000, whichever is the lower.

Netintra

Netintra has an outstanding invoice for £15,000, including VAT. The invoice is dated 1 March. Netintra has often been slow to pay in the past, and has now given several excuses to delay payment, ranging from being unable to trace any of the original documentation to the authorised cheque signatory being away. Softfruit has supplied Netintra with copies of all relevant documentation and, in accordance with the credit control policy, is now about to instruct a debt collection agency or commence legal action.

The HR director has asked you to refrain from sending the debt collectors or instructing solicitors because the Managing Director of Netintra is president of the local tennis club. She wishes to join this club, and she is concerned that any unpleasant tension will affect her application.

Softfruit has had some problems with certain customer accounts following a computer virus. The accounts department has managed to recover the following details relating to the account of Megachips:

- Balance at 1 May: £65,000 (debit)

- Invoices raised: 5 May £22,000 net of VAT, 12 June £16,920 including VAT

- Credit notes issued: 17 May £3,840 including VAT, 14 June £2,100 including VAT

- Late payment charge processed in May relating to an overdue invoice from February: £250

- Balance at 31 May: £37,600 (debit)

- Balance at 30 June: £2,100 (credit)

(b) Calculate the payments received from Megachips in May and in June.

AAT AQ2016 SAMPLE ASSESSMENT 1 CREDIT MANAGEMENT

ANSWERS

Credit Management (CDMT)
AAT sample assessment 1

Task 1 (18 marks)

(a) **Drag and drop the correct words into the following statement.**

Terms specifically stated in a contract are known as ⌐express¬ terms, which are ⌐binding¬ for both parties. Terms that are fundamental to a contract are known as ⌐conditions¬. If they are broken, the party breaking them will be in breach of contract and can be sued for ⌐damages¬.

(b) **What is the amount of interest that Holst may charge Gustav under the Late Payment of Commercial Debts (Interest) Act? Calculate your answer to the nearest penny.**

£ | 628.77

(c) **Identify whether the following statements about the Data Protection Act are true or false.**

	True ✓	False ✓
Companies are able to find out what information is held about them on computer-based records.		✓
Individuals have a right to object to decisions taken where there is no human involvement.	✓	
Individuals cannot request that data relating to them will not be used for direct marketing purposes.		✓
Data cannot be kept for more than six months.		✓

Sanjay orders 500 sweaters from an online fashion supplier. The sweaters are described as 100% wool. When the sweaters arrive. Sanjay checks the labels and sees that the material is described as 50% wool, 50% man-made fibres.

(d) **The contract between Sanjay and the fashion supplier is voidable due to:**

	✓
Unfair Contract	
Fraud	
Misrepresentation	✓
Consumer Credit	

(e) **Identify whether the following statements about consideration in contract law are true or false.**

Consideration has to be in the form of goods or money.	False
Consideration can be in the form of agreeing to perform an existing public duty.	False
Consideration can be a promise to do something in the future.	True

Task 2 (24 marks)

(a) **Complete the table below by calculating the key indicators (to two decimal places) for 20X5 and 20X4 for Bathrooms Ltd, and rate the company using the credit rating scoring system.**

Bathrooms Ltd	20X5 Indicator	20X5 Rating	20X4 Indicator	20X4 Rating
Operating profit margin %	4.89	0	−1.46	−5
Interest cover	2.42	0	−1.20	−30
Current ratio	1.20	−10	1.20	−10
Gearing %	51.79	0	37.62	10
Total credit rating		−10		−35

(b) **Based on the results of your credit rating and using the table above, recommend whether the requested credit limit should be given to Bathrooms Ltd.**

Customer	Decision
Bathrooms Ltd	Request latest management accounts and defer decision

Task 3 (30 marks)

(a) **Write notes to brief a new member of the credit control team explaining three sources of external information you will use (other than financial statements) when assessing whether to grant credit to a new customer. Comment on the role of the sales director in the credit assessment process.**

> There are a wide variety of sources which can be used when assessing the granting of credit, both internal and external. We will usually try to use a combination of sources in order to try to get the fullest picture of whether a new customer is an acceptable credit risk.
>
> External sources of information include bank references, trade references, credit rating agencies, credit circles, and industry/trade publications. Bank references must be interpreted carefully, as banks have a duty of confidentiality. Their first regard is to their own customer and references are therefore usually worded in fairly standard ways – and we must try to interpret the 'real' meaning behind this. Banks will only give an opinion on the overall soundness of the customer and will not be able to tell us how quickly they might pay their debts.
>
> Trade references are responses from other companies who have dealt with the prospective customer and may be able to tell us something about the payment profile. However, it is important to bear in mind that the customer themselves has nominated these references and may have selected only those who might reply favourably.
>
> Credit rating/reference agencies are organisations who maintain databases of information about individuals and businesses. The amount of information can be detailed (eg payment history, bankruptcy proceedings, court judgements etc) but can be out of date.
>
> Credit Circles are groups of businesses in the same type of industry who have customers in common with each other and who meet on a regular basis. The sharing of information (often on an informal basis) can give useful and timely information on any possible problems with customers.
>
> Trade publications and the media can sometimes be useful when considering the type of business a potential customer is in, and can help to see what overall trade views are on specific businesses, although it is important to check the facts behind any opinions provided in articles.
>
> The sales director should have minimal input when assessing whether to grant credit. Whilst she may be knowledgeable about the industry, her role is to increase sales and undertake marketing activities and she may not be knowledgeable about the process of credit control and the importance of liquidity and credit management.
>
> In any event, the sales director's role is primarily sales driven, and she may be influenced by the fact that she receives a bonus based on the amount of new business.

(b) **Write a note analysing the information and recommending whether credit should be granted.**

Profitability

The turnover has decreased by a small amount (3.5%).

There is no real explanation for this – perhaps just a small downturn in the market which can be monitored.

The gross profit has fallen by a similar amount (3.1%) and £190,000 in absolute terms.

The operating profit margin has fallen by 25% or £770,000 in absolute terms.

This fall in profitability may be because Berlin has changed its method of acquiring non-current assets and it may initially be more expensive to deal with the operating leases.

This may be a concern in the future if the admin and distribution expenses have a large fixed element. Interest cover appears to be healthy and has improved, but this is due to the reduction in finance lease costs not due to an increase in operating profit. The business is less reliant on finance leases but is relying on operating leases.

Liquidity

The current ratio is higher than the previous year meaning liquidity appears to have improved. The receivables collection period has decreased by nearly 2 days and is around an average of 30 days, which is a standard term of trade for many companies.

This gives some assurance that Berlin is managing its debt collection as well as in prior years. Inventory also appears to be being managed adequately as the amount has fallen both in absolute terms and in inventory holding days.

A similar comment may be made about trade payables, so it seems that working capital is being managed relatively efficiently.

Gearing and risk

The gearing has decreased from 77.75% to 47.27%, which would seem to give great comfort. The absolute level of borrowing has reduced substantially from £12.7 million to £4.325 million. This is a good sign.

However, the commitments under operating leases need to be considered as this is similar to debt. The annual operating lease commitments are almost £12 million which must be considered as financing.

The operating leases are non-cancellable, which means that the risk attached to this is quite high, particularly if the equipment is not hired out on a regular basis.

If this were included as borrowing in the balance sheet the gearing would be deemed to be extremely high.

Conclusion

In general the performance indicators seem acceptable. Although there has been a decline in profitability, the business is still making a profit and manages its working capital well. The main issue is assessing the impact of the operating leases, and whether this Is sustainable if Berlin faces a fall in equipment hire or other sales.

This might require an understanding of future forecasts for the industry, but it would certainly be appropriate to ask Berlin about future cash now projections.

A decision on granting credit should therefore be deferred until after suitable discussions with Berlin and the provision of further up to date management Information.

If credit is to be granted, further comfort in the way of retention of title clauses, credit insurance or directors' guarantees might be considered.

Task 4 (20 marks)

Complete the email to the chief credit controller, calculating and commenting on key ratios, and conclude by recommending whether or not credit should be extended. All calculations should be given to to two decimal in places.

Email

To: Credit Controller **Date:** Today

From: AAT Technician **Subject:** New Customer Thyme Ltd

Please find below my calculations, observations and recommendation for new customer Thyme Ltd.

Profitability

Turnover has increased by $\boxed{43.13\%}$. Gross profit margin in 20X4 was $\boxed{36.49}$ % and $\boxed{28.86}$ % in 20X5.

Operating profit itself has increased by $\boxed{33.65\%}$, however the operating profit margin in 20X5 was $\boxed{13.48}$ % as compared to $\boxed{14.23}$ % in 20X4. This means that $\boxed{\text{expenses have been well controlled}}$ although there might be some signs of possible $\boxed{\text{overtrading}}$ which need to be investigated further.

Interest can be covered $\boxed{\text{over 6 times}}$ in both years.

Liquidity

Both the current ratio and the quick (acid test) ratio have ▢ deteriorated ▢. In order to understand the liquidity position further it is important to review the trade cycles and the individual components making up the ratios.

Inventory has increased by ▢ 101.39 ▢ %. When compared to the increase in turnover this might indicate that Thyme is planning further increases in sales. The inventory holding period has increased from ▢ 60.12 ▢ days in 20X4 to ▢ 76.46 ▢ days in 20X5.

This means that ▢ funds are tied up in inventory ▢.

The trade receivables collection period has ▢ worsened by over 20 days ▢. Trade receivables have increased by ▢ 90.19% ▢.

This might mean that ▢ Thyme is offering more generous terms to encourage ▢.

The payables payment period is ▢ significantly more than ▢ our standard terms of trade.

The company has no cash in 20X5 and is more reliant on ▢ short-term borrowing ▢.

Recommendation

I recommend that ▢ we refuse any credit. ▢

136

Task 5 (22 marks)

(a) **Match each type or claim on the left to the appropriate type of court procedure on the right.** *(CBT instruction: Click on the left box first then on the corresponding right box. You can remove a line by clicking on it.)*

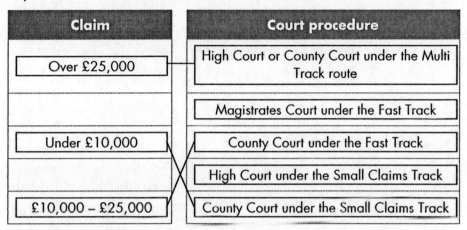

Claim	Court procedure
Over £25,000	High Court or County Court under the Multi Track route
	Magistrates Court under the Fast Track
Under £10,000	County Court under the Fast Track
	High Court under the Small Claims Track
£10,000 – £25,000	County Court under the Small Claims Track

(b) **Which of the following statements are true if a retention of title claim is to be successfully enforced?**

	True	False
The goods subject to the clause must be clearly identifiable.	✓	
Goods which have been altered cannot usually be repossessed.	✓	
The goods subject to the clause must be in the customer's warehouse.		✓
There must be a rentention of title clause shown on every invoice sent to the customer.		✓

(c) **Complete the following sentences.**

ABC is offering [a recourse factoring facility] .

XYZ can borrow: [£ | 1,750,000] .

(d) **Which of the following are stages in a company winding up procedure?**

(i)   Statutory demand
(ii)   Petition to the Court
(iii)   Bankruptcy order
(iii)   Appointment or Administrator

	✓
(i), (ii) and (iii)	
(i) and (ii)	✓
All of the above	
(ii) and (iv)	

(e) **Drag and drop the correct words into the following statement.**

An aged receivables analysis is a management tool that can be used to highlight customers who are $\boxed{\text{slow to pay}}$.

It analyses the balance due from each customer according to the $\boxed{\text{date}}$ of each invoice outstanding.

Analysis of trade receivables can also be undertaken based on focusing attention on $\boxed{20\%}$ of customer accounts which make up $\boxed{80\%}$ of the total value of outstanding debts.

Christopher owes Jayne £7,500 for goods supplied.

(f) **What is the normal remedy for Jayne as a result of non payment of the debt?**

	✓
Action for breach	
Action for price	✓
Specific injunction	
Action for restitution	

Task 6 (16 marks)

DEF Ltd wishes to claim VAT bad debt relief on some unpaid customer invoices.

(a) **Identify whether each statement below is true or false.**

In order for DEF Ltd to be able to successfully reclaim VAT on an unpaid debt:

	True or False
DEF Ltd must have already accounted for the VAT and paid it over to HMRC	True
The claim must be made within three years of the due date of payment of the debt	False
DEF Ltd must have made a provision for the unpaid debt	False
The debt must have remained unpaid for six months after the due date of payment	True

Meerkat Ltd wishes to offer a 2% discount to its customers for settlement of invoices within 21 days. Meerkat's standard terms of trade are 45 days.

(b) **Calculate the following to two decimal places:**

The simple annual cost of the discount ⌐31.04⌐ %

The compound annual cost of the discount ⌐35.97⌐ %

(c) **Which ONE of the following is an important aspect of liquidity management?**

	✓
Having enough assets to meet all obligations on a timely basis.	
Being able to pay all suppliers and other operational costs as they fall due.	✓
Being profitable enough to settle amounts due when they become payable.	
Rescheduling loan repayments to ensure they are non-current liabilities.	

Jonty's customers currently pay 30 days after the month end. He is introducing a 1% discount from month 2 if customers settle the invoice in the same month. It is expected that 80% of customers will take advantage of this. The expected sales revenue per month is as follows:

	Sales revenue £
Month 1	95,000
Month 2	105,000
Month 3	136,000

(d) **Expected cash receipts in month 3 will be:**

£ | 128,712

(e) **Which ONE or the following is NOT a type of credit insurance?**

	✓
Key account	
Catastrophe	
Unlimited excess	✓
Whole turnover	

Tom has received a letter from the liquidator of Jerry Ltd. The liquidator has indicated that all unsecured creditors of Jerry will receive a dividend of 2.5p in the pound (£) later in the year. Tom is owed £7,500 by Jerry.

(f) **Calculate the amount that Tom should write off as an irrecoverable debt. Ignore VAT. Show your answer to the nearest penny.**

£ | 7,312.50

Task 7 (20 marks)

(a) **Review the information provided for each customer below and prepare comments and an action plan for dealing with the outstanding amounts due to Softfruit. Your action plan should include a summary of the options available to Softfruit to pursue outstanding amounts, along with recommendations for provisions or write off of irrecoverable debts where appropriate.**

FDP

FDP is a regular customer of Softfruit and always pays to terms. FDP is responsible for 15% of Softfruits annual turnover. FDP had ordered 12 custom-built computers for use in a new software development project. The order had specified that all 12 computers were to be delivered by 16 April in time for the project to begin. Softfruit delivered six computers on 15 April. However, due to the extended illness of their computer engineer Softfruit could only deliver the remaining six computers on 25 April.

The total value of the invoice to FDP dated 25 April is £72,000 including VAT. FDP has complained about the late delivery, stating that this has significantly delayed their important project. They are withholding payment and asking for compensation.

Care needs to be taken here as FDP seems to be a customer who places regular orders and provides Softfruit with a substantial part of their sales – a tactful approach is therefore required. The terms of the sale contract need to be reviewed carefully, as well as delivery documentation, as FDP are possibly in breach of contract if the delivery date was part of the agreed terms.

Even though part of the order was delivered on time, the remainder was 10 days late. If Softfruit were determined to be in breach of contract, they would be liable for damages. The amount of damages would be determined based on what FDP might have incurred by way of costs or lost revenue as a result of the delay.

It would therefore be preferable to meet with FDP and negotiate some kind of discount for the problems and inconvenience caused. This would avoid any legal costs, maintain customer goodwill and hopefully bring about payment of the outstanding amount less any discount. As FDP has always otherwise paid to terms, there is no reason to make any provision or take other action to collect the debt at this point.

Gigabits

Softfruit has received notification that Gigabits is in receivership. The amount of the outstanding debt is £28,620 including VAT. The receiver has told Softfruit that she will not accept any retention of title claim as the goods in question are generic computer components that Gigabits has purchased from a number of suppliers. It will therefore not be possible to identify which had been supplied by Softfruit.

The account is credit insured for a maximum of 75% of the net debt or £15,000, whichever is the lower.

A receiver will often attempt to reject ROT claims in the first instance therefore Softfruit should check what sort of goods they have recently supplied to Gigabits. If the goods are small components then the receiver may be correct that it is not possible to identify which have been supplied by Softfruit, particularly if they had not been kept separate by Gigabits. However, it may be possible to identity Softfruit's components. Therefore if it is cost-effective to pay a visit to Gigabit's premises, Softfruit should send a representative immediately with all relevant documentation.

Softfruit has an 'all monies' retention of title clause. This means that it would not be necessary to match any goods unpaid for to specific outstanding invoices. If the ROT clause turns out to be unenforceable, Softfruit will be an unsecured creditor of Gigabits, which means it is unlikely that Softfruit will receive much, if any, of the outstanding amount.

A claim should be made on the credit insurance for the amount of £15,000. (Net debt is £28,620/1.2 = £23,850. Maximum claim is lower of £15,000 or 75% × £23,850 = £17,887.50). A provision should be made for the balance of £8,850. VAT of £4,770 can be reclaimed from HMRC after six months and after the debt has been written off.

Netintra

Netintra has an outstanding invoice for £15,000, including VAT. The invoice is dated 1 March. Netintra has often been slow to pay in the past, and has now given several excuses to delay payment, ranging from being unable to trace any of the original documentation to the authorised cheque signatory being away. Softfruit has supplied Netintra with copies of all relevant documentation and, in accordance with the credit control policy, is now about to instruct a debt collection agency or commence legal action.

The HR director has asked you to refrain from sending the debt collectors or instructing solicitors because the Managing Director of Netintra is president of the local tennis club. She wishes to join this club, and she is concerned that any unpleasant tension will affect her application.

Netintra seem to have used a variety of excuse and delaying tactics, while Softfruit has done its best to prove the amount owed. The debt is now substantially overdue (payment was due by 31 March, it is now 30 June, so the debt is 90 days old) with no apparent reason, even though Netintra are normally slow payers.

A credit control policy is in place to ensure that Softfruit does not suffer any unnecessary liquidity problems or unnecessary bad debts. Because there is no business reason for not pursuing the debt in accordance with the credit control policy, Softfruit should proceed to instruct a debt collection agency or commence legal action.

Causing 'unpleasantness' is not a sufficient reason for Softfruit not to protect its business position. The HR director's personal situation should have no bearing on Softfruit's business decisions and she should not use her position as a director to influence how a policy should be applied for her own personal gain.

(b) **Calculate the payments received from Megachips in May and in June.**

Megachips

	May £	June £
Opening balance	65,000	37,600
Invoice	26,400	16,920
Credit note	(3,840)	(2,100)
Interest charge	250	0
Closing balance	37,600	(2,100)
Payments received	**50,210**	**54,520**

AAT AQ2016 SAMPLE ASSESSMENT 2
Credit Management

You are advised to attempt sample assessment 2 online from the AAT website. This will ensure you are prepared for how the assessment will be presented on the AAT's system when you attempt the real assessment. Please access the assessment using the address below:

https://www.aat.org.uk/training/study-support/search

BPP PRACTICE ASSESSMENT 1
CREDIT MANAGEMENT

Time allowed: 2 hours and 30 minutes

Credit Management (CDMT)
BPP practice assessment 1

Task 1

(a) A cosmetics business produces and distributes a monthly catalogue to all the households in its local area to introduce its new products. The catalogue includes a price list and an order form. After a week the catalogues are collected along with any orders that have been placed.

Complete the following sentence.

In the terms of contract law the business's distribution of the catalogue is described as [⬛].

Picklist:

an intention to create legal relations
an invitation to treat
an offer

(b) Jane goes into the florist to buy some flowers that are advertised in the window as being on special offer at £5 a bunch. Inside the shop she finds that the advertised flowers are sold out and the cheapest bunches available are £7.50. Jane demands that the florist sell her the more expensive flowers at £5 but the florist refuses.

Which of the following statements is correct?

	✓
The advert is an invitation to treat and the florist's failure to make the advertised flowers available renders it a defective contract.	
The advert is an offer and the florist's failure to make the advertised flowers available is a breach of contract.	
The advert is an offer and Jane's demand that the florist sell her the more expensive flowers at £5 is a revocation of an offer.	
The advert is an invitation to treat and Jane's demand to buy the more expensive flowers at £5 is an offer which is rejected by the florist.	

(c) A business is owed £12,000 plus VAT at the standard rate. Currently the Bank of England base rate is 0.5% and the debt is 60 days late.

What is the amount of interest that the business may charge under the Late Payment of Commercial Debts (Interest) Act? Calculate your answer to the nearest penny.

£ ☐

(d) Consider the following statements made in connection with the Data Protection Act:

(i) 'Personal information' includes expressions of opinion as well as factual information held about a living individual.

(ii) A 'data subject' is a person who holds and processes personal information.

Which of the statements are true?

	✓
(i) only	
(ii) only	
Both statements	
Neither statement	

(e) Which of the following best describes consideration?

	✓
The payment of cash	
The promise of an exchange of value	
The intention for the parties to be legally bound	
The absolute and unqualified acceptance of both parties	

Task 2

Your company uses a credit rating system to assess the credit status of new customers.

The credit rating system table below is used to assess the risk of default by calculating key ratios, comparing them to the table and calculating an aggregate score.

	Score
Operating profit margin	
Loss	–2
Less than 4%	0
4% to 8%	2
Above 8%	4
Interest cover	
No cover	–2
Less than 1	0
Between 1 and 3	4
Over 3	

	Score
Current ratio	
Less than 1:1	–2
1:1 to 2:1	2
Over 2:1	4
Gearing (total debt/(total debt + equity))	
Less than 30%	4
Between 30% and 50%	2
Between 50% and 70%	0
Over 70%	–2

Risk assessment	Total score
Very low risk	16 to 20
Low risk	10 to 15
Medium risk	5 to 9
High risk	0 to 4
Very high risk	–10 to 0

Jemima Ltd is a potential new commercial customer which has previously bought goods from one of your competitors. Jemima Ltd wishes to open an account with your company with a credit limit of £10,000 and wants you to match your competitor's 60 day payment terms. The sales department are very keen to do business with Jemima Ltd and are exerting pressure on you to process the application quickly.

The following information relates to the application.

Jemima Ltd: Summarised Financial Statements year ended 30 November 20X7 and 20X6

Statement of profit or loss

	20X7	20X6
	£000	£000
Sales revenue	2,360	1,860
Cost of sales	1,690	1,560
Gross profit	670	300
Operating expenses	580	440
Profit from operations	90	(140)
Finance costs (interest payable)	40	10
Profit from operations before tax	50	(150)
Tax	12	0
Profit for the period	38	(150)

Jemima Ltd: Summarised statement of financial position at 30 November

	20X7 £000	20X6 £000
ASSETS		
Non-current assets	741	600
Current assets		
Inventory	280	270
Receivables	450	303
Cash at bank	2	4
	732	577
Total assets	**1,473**	**1,177**

	20X7 £000	20X6 £000
EQUITY AND LIABILITIES		
Equity		
Ordinary share capital	100	100
Retained earnings	315	277
Total equity	415	377
Non-current liabilities		
Long-term loans	600	400
Current liabilities		
Trade payables	370	350
Other payables	88	50
	458	400
Total liabilities	**1,058**	**800**
Total equity and liabilities	**1,473**	**1,177**

(a) **Complete the table below to show the key financial indicators (to two decimal places), scores and overall credit rating for 20X7 and 20X6.**

Jemima Ltd	20X7 Indicator	20X7 Score	20X6 Indicator	20X6 Score
Operating profit margin %				
Interest cover				
Current ratio				
Gearing %				
Total credit rating				

(b) **Based on your results of your credit rating recommend whether the requested credit limit should be given to Jemima Ltd.**

Customer	Decision
Jemima Ltd	▼

Picklist:

Accept
Reject

Task 3

When assessing the credit worthiness of new and existing customers various sources of information can be used. These sources of information can be categorised as internal and external information. A credit control colleague has now mentioned they are unsure of the types of internal information that can be used.

(a) **Write a brief note to your colleague explaining how internal information that can be used and when assessing an existing customer's credit increase request.**

Note

(b) Gofar Ltd is an existing customer and has contacted your company's sale team with a request to increase their credit limit from £50,000 to £100,000.

Gofar Ltd's credit period is 30 days and has supplied the following financial statements.

Gofar Ltd: Statement of financial position

	20X7 £000	20X6 £000
ASSETS		
Non-current assets		
Property, plant and equipment	12,000	10,000
Current assets		
Inventories	1,450	910
Trade and other receivables	2,030	1,638
Cash	5	10
	3,485	**2,558**
Total assets	**15,485**	**12,558**
EQUITY AND LIABILITIES		
Equity		
Share capital	1,000	1,000
Retained earnings	3,395	2,678
Total Equity	**4,395**	**3,678**
Non-current liabilities		
Borrowing	5,000	3,500
Current liabilities		
Trade and other payables	700	500
Taxation	100	200
Borrowing	5,290	4,680
	6,090	**5,380**
Total liabilities	**11,090**	**8,880**
Total equity and liabilities	**15,485**	**12,558**

Gofar Ltd: Statement of profit or loss

	20X7 £000	20X6 £000
Sales revenue	12,557	10,078
Cost of sales	9,765	5,618
Gross profit	**2,792**	**4,460**
Distribution costs	770	417
Administration expenses	825	483
Operating profit	**1,197**	**3,560**
Finance costs	160	120
Profit before taxation	**1,037**	**3,440**
Taxation	320	700
Profit for the year	**717**	**2,740**

Gofar Ltd: Key financial indicators

	20X7	20X6
Gross profit margin %	22.23	44.25
Operating profit margin %	9.53	35.32
Interest cover	7.48	29.67
Current ratio	0.38	0.35
Trade payables payment period in days	26.16	32.48
Trade receivables collection period in days	59.00	59.32
Inventory holding period in days	54.19	59.12
Gearing %	70.10	68.98

Additional information:

1. Gofar Ltd is a furniture manufacturer and sells directly to the public through large stores located in retail parks.

2. During the last 12 months the company has been pursuing a strategy of heavy sales price discounts.

3. In attempt to increase market share further stores have been purchased and these have been financed by bank borrowing.

Using the above information compose a note to your company's chief credit controller analysing whether the requested credit increase should be granted or declined.

Note

Task 4

A potential new customer Jandata Ltd wishes to make an order for £25,000 and has sent in financial statements for two years in support of their request.

Jandata Ltd: Statement of profit or loss

	20X7	20X6
Sales revenue	3,965	4,125
Cost of sales	3,020	3,160
Gross profit	**945**	**965**
Distribution costs	415	480
Administration expenses	**455**	**525**
Operating profit	**75**	**(40)**
Finance costs	150	100
Profit before taxation	**(75)**	**(140)**
Taxation	0	0
Profit for the year	**(75)**	**(140)**

Jandata Ltd: Statement of financial position

	20X7 £000	20X6 £000
Assets		
Non-current assets		
Property, plant and equipment	2,200	1,775
Current assets		
Inventories	550	600
Trade and other receivables	640	570
Cash	80	400
	1,270	**1,570**
Total assets	**3,470**	**3,345**
Equity and liabilities		
Equity		
Share capital	600	600
Retained earnings	545	670
Total Equity	**1,145**	**1,270**
Non-current liabilities		
Borrowing	1,400	1,200
Current liabilities		
Borrowing	120	100
Trade and other payables	805	775
Total liabilities	**2,325**	**2,075**
Total equity and liabilities	**3,470**	**3,345**

Complete the following memo (using the picklists or entering a number to the nearest whole number) assessing the financial statements of Jandata Ltd and reach a conclusion on whether the credit request should be granted or rejected.

The credit controller has informed you that for this company both current and non-current borrowings are treated as debt and also a part of capital employed.

Memo

To: Credit controller

Subject: Credit request from Jandata Ltd

Further to the request from Jandata Ltd for £25,000 of credit I have analysed the information that has been available to us for the last two years.

Profitability

The gross profit margin for the two years has (1) [▼] and the gross margin

percentage for 20X7 was [   ] %. In 20X6 there was an operating

(2) [▼] and in 20X7 the operating profit margin was [   ] %.

Liquidity

In 20X6 the current ratio was [   ] and in 20X7 the current ratio was

[   ] this means this key liquidity ratio has (3) [▼] over the two

years. In 20X6 the trade payables period was [   ] days and in 20X7 this

had (3) [▼] to [   ] days. This means (4)

[▼]

Picklist:

(1) decreased
     increased

(2) loss
     profit

(3) decreased
     increased

(4) Jandata Ltd is a prompt payer to suppliers
     Jandata Ltd is taking longer to pay suppliers

Gearing

Gearing in 20X6 was [_____] % and in 20X7 [_____] %. This indicates that gearing is (1) [_____ ▼] and is a (2) [_____ ▼] sign as the company is (3) [_____ ▼] reliant on bank finance to keep trading.

Conclusion

Taking into account the profitability of the company and trend in the gearing ratio my recommendation is that we (4) [_____ ▼] the £25,000 credit limit request.

Picklist:

(1) decreased
     increased

(2) negative
     positive

(3) less
     more

(4) accept
     decline

Task 5

(a) Alpha Limited has supplied goods on credit to a self-employed plumber, but the debt of £800 remains unpaid, despite issuing a statutory demand for payment.

From this stage the next step Alpha Ltd can approach the Court for
[_____ ▼].

Picklist:

an attachment of earnings order
a petition for bankruptcy
appointment of a liquidator
appointment of an insolvency practitioner

(b) **What does the Late Payment of Commercial Debts Act allow?**

	✓
A supplier must offer a purchaser a settlement discount	
A supplier can insist upon a settlement discount being taken by a purchaser	
A purchaser can only pay for goods after the credit term if agreed with the supplier	
A supplier can charge interest on overdue amounts owing	

(c) **Conrad Ltd is refusing to pay an outstanding invoice of £5,500 to Wiggins plc.**

The [▼] would deal with any legal action brought by Wiggins plc to enforce payment of the debt.

Picklist:

County Court – Fast Track
County Court – Small Claims Track
High Court – Multi Track
Industrial tribunal

(d) **Which of the following services is unlikely to be available from a debt factoring company?**

	✓
Administration of the receivables ledger	
An advance of finance in respect of a certain percentage of receivables	
Insurance against irrecoverable debts	
Seizure of property from customers who refuse to pay	

(e) A garage entered into a contract to purchase petrol. This supply later turned out to be diesel and until this was discovered a number of petrol engines have been ruined.

The most appropriate remedy for the garage against their supplier would be

[▼].

Picklist:

action for the price
monetary damages
quantum meruit
specific performance

(f) A customer's outstanding balance as at 31 December 20X1 has been analysed as follows:

19/09/X1	Invoice 175	£610
23/09/X1	Invoice 177	£667
23/09/X1	Credit note for goods returned	–£31
10/10/X1	Invoice 178	£894
21/11/X1	Invoice 179	£561
Balance outstanding		**£2,701**

What is the mount that would appear in the aged receivables analysis as more than 90 days outstanding?

	✓
£1,246	
£1,308	
£2,140	
£2,202	

Task 6

(a) A company's standard credit terms are 30 days. The company is considering offering a 2% discount for payment within 10 days.

Calculate the following stating your answers to two decimal places.

The simple cost of the discount [ ] %

The compound annual cost of the discount [ ] %

(b) Before VAT bad debt relief can be claimed the debt needs to be outstanding for [ ]

Picklist:

1 month
3 months
6 months

A business intends to claim VAT bad debt relief for an overdue debt amounting to £10,440 including VAT at the standard rate of 20%.

Calculate the VAT that can be reclaimed.

£ [ ]

(c) **Complete the following statement.**

[ ] is not a recognised type of credit insurance.

Picklist:

Annual aggregate excess policy
Specific receivables
Third party policy
Whole turnover policy

(d) Barney plc has taken out a credit insurance policy to claim for unpaid customer accounts. The policy allows claims up to 90% of the value of any debts claimed for. One of Barney's customers, Fred is now bankrupt and owes £2,880 including VAT at 20%. The debt is over two years old and Barney plc intends to claim for VAT bad debt relief.

Calculate the amount Barney plc should write-off as irrecoverable.

£ [ ]

(e) **Which of the following is the correct description of a credit circle?**

	✓
A commercial organisation which provides credit status information about companies and individuals	
The time taken between a business paying for its raw materials and receiving cash in from the customer for the sale of the product	
A group of companies, often operating in the same industry, who share information on current and prospective customers for credit purposes	
The steps that a business goes through between the customer receiving an invoice for a credit sale and cash being received by the business	

(f) A business has generated an aged receivables' report for all customers as at 1 June 20X1.

Total £	Current < 30 days £	30–60 days £	>60 days £
404,000	115,000	126,000	163,000

Payment profile for June:

(1) 20% of >60 days to pay in full
(2) 60% of 30–60 days to settle less a discount of 1%
(3) 80% of <30 days to settle less a discount of 2%

Calculate the expected receipts in June.

£

Task 7

You are responsible for reviewing your company's aged receivables analysis and you have received the following exception report along with associated notes.

Exception report as at 31 March 20X6

Customer	Note	Credit terms	Credit limit £	Amount due £	Current £	31–60 days £	61–90 days £
Roxy plc	1	45 days	50,000.00	13,250.00	11,000.00		2,250
Flames Ltd	2	60 days	25,000.00	16,815.75	6,815.75	7,500	2,500
Ice Ltd	3	60 days	25,000.00	10,000.00			10,000

Notes

(1) Roxy plc – Dispute the invoice for £2,250, claiming never to have received the goods concerned. The signed delivery note cannot be traced. They are a regular customer and represent 20% of your company's sales revenue. Normally there are no problems dealing with Roxy plc and the rest of the account is up to date.

(2) Flames Ltd – The invoice for £2,500 is dated 28 January 20X6. It has been reported in the press that one of Flames Ltd's major customers has recently gone into liquidation and that Flames Ltd are experiencing cash flow difficulties as a result. This account is not credit insured and is not in dispute.

(3) Ice Ltd – Since this one specific order of £10,000 a year ago there has been no further orders made from Ice Ltd. The company has not responded to chasing letters and there is no answer when telephoned. The account is credit insured up to 90% of its value and the amount outstanding includes VAT at the standard rate.

(a) Review each of the three customers and complete the tables below discussing appropriate actions to take including whether any amounts should be provided for as doubtful or written-off as irrecoverable.

Roxy plc

Flames Ltd

Ice Ltd

(b) Your sales ledger information needs to be entered manually on to a new accounting system to calculate customer balances at 30 April and 31 May 20X6.

The following information is available:

Balance

1 April 20X6 – £1,800

Invoice raised

5 April 20X6 – £2,000 plus VAT at 20%
16 May 20X6 – £4,000 VAT inclusive

Credit notes raised

18 April 20X6 – £120 (VAT inclusive)
24 May 20X6 – £240 (VAT inclusive) Less £40 restocking fee

Bank receipts

20 April 20X6 – £1,950
28 May 20X6 – £3,750

Calculate the closing balances as at 30 April 20X6 and 31 May 20X6.

BPP PRACTICE ASSESSMENT 1
CREDIT MANAGEMENT

ANSWERS

Credit Management (CDMT)
BPP practice assessment 1

Task 1

(a) In the terms of contract law the business's distribution of the catalogue is described as | an invitation to treat |.

(b)

	✓
The advert is an invitation to treat and the florist's failure to make the advertised flowers available renders it a defective contract.	
The advert is an offer and the florist's failure to make the advertised flowers available is a breach of contract.	
The advert is an offer and Jane's demand that the florist sell her the more expensive flowers at £5 is a revocation of an offer.	
The advert is an invitation to treat and Jane's demand to buy the more expensive flowers at £5 is an offer which is rejected by the florist.	✓

(c)

£	201.20

(d)

	✓
(i) only	✓
(ii) only	
Both statements	
Neither statement	

(e)

	✓
The payment of cash	
The promise of an exchange of value	✓
The intention for the parties to be legally bound	
The absolute and unqualified acceptance of both parties	

Task 2

(a)

Jemima Ltd	20X7 Indicator	20X7 Score	20X6 Indicator	20X6 Score
Operating profit margin %	3.81	0	–7.53	–2
Interest cover	2.25	4	Nil	–2
Current ratio	1.60	2	1.44	2
Gearing %	59.11	0	51.48	0
Total credit rating		6		–4

(b)

Customer	Decision
Jemima Ltd	Accept

Credit request accepted as Jemima Ltd has achieved a medium risk score in latest year.

Task 3

(a)

Note

When reaching credit decisions it is always prudent to use as many different sources of information as possible. This approach reduces the risk associated when relying on one or two sources of information only. This is because limited information can be incorrect or out of date so that an incorrect conclusion is reached.

Broadly there are two sources of information and these are external and internal sources.

Internal sources can be of the most reliable and cost effective of information sources and these include; staff knowledge, customer visits and also internal analysis of aged receivable reports and interpretation of customer financial statements.

Staff knowledge

Staff and colleagues who are dealing with customers on a day-to-day basis can build a close relationship with customers and this can be invaluable when considering a customer's credit facility. Staff who have contact with customers can have a good idea on whether the customer is doing well or in financial difficulties. Indications can be any changes in key staff within a customer's business or the business's standing and reputation in the market place.

Customer visits

Feedback from staff visits to customer's premises can be useful in gaining a picture on the credit worthiness of a business. Positive signs can include a good morale with the customer's staff and busy shop or office. Negative signs can include a disorganised premises or observation of dissatisfaction for their own customers or staff.

Analysis of aged receivables reports or customer financial statements

Regular reviews of aged receivables reports can help to identify customers who are paying on time and staying within their agreed credit limits. Such reviews can also highlight late payers, and customers with irregular payment patterns. Analysis of a customer's financial statements can be helpful in many ways through analysis of indicators and ratios. These can fall under the following three headings; profitability, liquidity and gearing. The credit control function can then devise and apply a scoring system using these calculations to rate the riskiness of a customer. This enables an objective credit assessment decision to be reached.

(b)

Note

To: Chief Credit Controller,

Please find an analysis below on whether Gofar Ltd's credit request should be granted or declined.

Profitability

The gross profit margin has decreased from 44.25% to 22.23% and as Gofar Ltd is discounting its goods this indicates that this due from cuts in selling prices. Sales revenue has increased from £10,078,000 in 20X6 up to £12,557,000 in 20X7 and this must mean that there is an increase in unit volume encouraged by the sales price discounts and opening of new stores.

The operating profit margin has decreased dramatically between 20X6 and 20X7. This can be partly attributed to the decrease in the gross profit margin but looking at the absolute figures; 20X6: £770,000 and £825,000, 20X7: £417,000 and £483,000 shows that distribution costs and administration costs have increased by nearly 80% indicating poor cost control.

Consequently profit for the year has decreased from £2,740,000 down to £717,000.

Liquidity

The current ratio has been consistent between the two years however this may be considered low for this type of business at around only 35p or 38p of current assets for every £1 of current liabilities. Customers are taking around 60 days to settle their accounts and this can put pressure on the availability of cash to pay Gofar Ltd's suppliers. Inventory is turning over on an approximately 2 month basis and it may be some concern that inventory is slow to move even though the company is increasing unit volume. Cash in hand has dropped by 50% from £10,000 to £5,000 and can indicate there can be a lack of cash to pay immediate bills.

Gearing

Gearing can be considered higher than average at around 70%. Long term borrowing has increased up to £5,000,000 and this may be due to investment in new stores. Finance costs have risen accordingly and this has been reflected in a decrease in interest cover. The drop in interest cover is also due to the decrease in operating profits from 20X6 to 20X7. The company is using a mixture of short term and long term borrowing and may be using revolving short term finance to support its long term finance requirements.

Conclusion

Looking at the drop in profitability and pressure on liquidity it appears that Gofar Ltd is overtrading and the credit increase request should be declined at the present time.

Task 4

Memo

To: Credit controller
Subject: Credit request from Jandata Ltd

Further to the request from Jandata Ltd for £25,000 of credit I have analysed the information that has been available to us for the last two years.

Profitability

The gross profit margin for the two years has [increased] and the gross margin percentage for 20X7 was [23.83] %. In 20X6 there was an operating [loss] and in 20X7 the operating profit margin was [1.89] %.

Liquidity

In 20X6 the current ratio was [1.79] and in 20X7 the current ratio was [1.37] this means this key liquidity ratio has [decreased] over the two years. In 20X6 the trade payables period was [89] days and in 20X7 this had [increased] to [97] days. This means [Jandata Ltd is taking longer to pay suppliers].

Gearing

Gearing in 20X6 was [50.58] % and in 20X7 [57.04] %. This indicates that gearing is [increased] and is a [negative] sign as the company is [more] reliant on bank finance to keep trading.

Conclusion

Taking into account the profitability of the company and trend in the gearing ratio my recommendation is that we [decline] the £25,000 credit limit request.

Task 5

(a) From this stage the next step Alpha Ltd can approach the Court for
| a petition for bankruptcy | .

(b)

	✓
A supplier must offer a purchaser a settlement discount	
A supplier can insist upon a settlement discount being taken by a purchaser	
A purchaser can only pay for goods after the credit term if agreed with the supplier	
A supplier can charge interest on overdue amounts owing	✓

(c) The | County Court – Small Claims Track | would deal with any legal action brought by Wiggins plc to enforce payment of the debt.

(d)

	✓
Administration of the receivables ledger	
An advance of finance in respect of a certain percentage of receivables	
Insurance against irrecoverable debts	
Seizure of property from customers who refuse to pay	✓

(e) The most appropriate remedy for the garage against their supplier would be
| monetary damages | .

(f)

	✓
£1,246	✓
£1,308	
£2,140	
£2,202	

Task 6

(a) The simple cost of the discount $\boxed{37.24}$ %

The compound annual cost of the discount $\boxed{44.56}$ %

(b) Before VAT bad debt relief can be claimed the debt needs to be outstanding for $\boxed{6 \text{ months}}$

The VAT that can be reclaimed is:

£ $\boxed{1,740}$

(c) $\boxed{\text{Third party policy}}$ is not a recognised type of credit insurance.

(d) The amount Barney plc should write-off as irrecoverable is:

£ $\boxed{240}$

(e)

	✓
A commercial organisation which provides credit status information about companies and individuals	
The time taken between a business paying for its raw materials and receiving cash in from the customer for the sale of the product	
A group of companies, often operating in the same industry, who share information on current and prospective customers for credit purposes	✓
The steps that a business goes through between the customer receiving an invoice for a credit sale and cash being received by the business	

(f) The expected receipts in June amount to:

£ $\boxed{197,604}$

Task 7

(a) Roxy plc

As Roxy plc is a large customer care needs to be taken not to risk a profitable business relationship. As the delivery note cannot be located it can be possible that Roxy plc did not in fact receive the goods as stated. We could try to obtain additional information from the delivery driver to see if a delivery took place and also look at supporting ordering documents. Retention of title clauses will not help here as Roxy plc may not have received the goods. Until we can internally confirm that the goods were actually delivered no legal or other action should be taken. As the amount is relatively small we should continue trading until this issue has been resolved. No allowance for doubtful debts are needed at the time being as the customer is still trading and is up to date with other transactions. If it is found that the goods were not delivered then a credit note can be raised for the £2,250 and a letter of apology sent to Roxy plc.

Flames Ltd

As this customer owes money from 90 days plus this account should be put on stop with immediate effect and no further orders accepted. As this account is not credit insured we need to consider whether to instruct a solicitor or debt collection agency to chase this debt. The amounts are not in dispute so an appropriate action can be to instruct a solicitor to send a legal letter requesting payment. If payment is not forthcoming then stronger action will need to be taken as legally Flames Ltd are in breach of contract. There have been some negative reports surrounding Flames Ltd and it would be prudent to create an allowance for doubtful debts until either the debt is settled with a view to write-off as irrecoverable if payment is not received.

Ice Ltd

Ice Ltd has no current trading and owes for one order made some time ago. This account needs to be put on stop and no further orders to be accepted. As the account is credit insured a claim needs to be made for 90% of the net amount of the invoice. As the debt is over 6 months old the VAT can be claimed back from HMRC through VAT bad debt relief. Any amounts that cannot be reclaimed need to be written off a irrecoverable.

(b)

> **April**
>
> | | |
> |---|---|
> | Opening balance | £1,800 |
> | Plus April's invoice | £2,400 (inc VAT) |
> | Less April's credit note | (£120) |
> | Less April's bank receipts | (£1,950) |
> | Closing balance c/d | **£2,130** |
>
> **May**
>
> | | |
> |---|---|
> | Opening balance b/d | £2,130 |
> | Plus May's invoice | £4,000 |
> | Less May's net credit note | (£200) |
> | Less May's bank receipts | (£3,750) |
> | Closing balance c/d | **£2,180** |

BPP PRACTICE ASSESSMENT 2
CREDIT MANAGEMENT

Time allowed: 2 hours and 30 minutes

Credit Management (CDMT)
BPP practice assessment 2

Task 1

(a) **Which of the following is not an essential element of a valid simple contract?**

	✓
The contract must be in writing	
The parties must be in agreement	
Each party must provide consideration	
Each party must intend legal relations	

Complete the following sentence.

(b) [▾] is a normal remedy for breach of contract due to non-payment of a debt.

Picklist:

An action for the goods
An action for the price
Quantum meruit
Specific performance

(c) **The Consumer Rights Act 2015 implies a number of terms into consumer contracts. Which of the following are terms it implies?**

	✓
Title, quantity, fitness	
Title, sale by sample, price	
Description, price, fitness	
Description, quality, fitness	

(d) **Complete the following sentence.**

Misrepresentation results in a contract being [▼] .

Picklist:

invalid
valid
void
voidable

(e) **Consider the following statements:**

(i) A data controller can be either an individual or a company.

(ii) Data is subject to the Data Protection Act's regulation, if it merely records the holder's opinion about the subject, rather than facts about him or her.

Which statements are true?

	✓
(i) only	
(ii) only	
Both statements	
Neither statement	

Task 2

You work as a credit control manager for Collins Ltd which uses a credit rating system to assess the credit status of new customers.

The credit rating system table below is used to assess the risk of default by calculating key ratios, comparing them to the table and calculating an aggregate score. The key ratios used are operating profit margin, current ratio, accounts payable payment period, gearing and interest cover.

Credit rating system	Score
Operating profit margin	
Loss	–2
Less than 4%	0
4% to 8%	2
Above 8%	4

Credit rating system	Score
Current ratio	
Less than 1 : 1	–2
1 : 1 to 2 : 1	2
Over 2 : 1	4
Accounts payable payment period	
Up to 30 days	4
30 to 45 days	2
45 to 60 days	0
Over 60 days	–2
Gearing (total debt/(total debt + equity))	
Less than 30%	4
Between 30% and 50%	2
Between 50% and 70%	0
Over 70%	–2
Interest cover	
No cover	–2
Less than 1	0
Between 1 and 3	2
Over 3	4
Risk assessment	
Very low risk	16 to 20
Low risk	10 to 15
Medium risk	5 to 9
High risk	0 to 4
Very high risk	–10 to 0

The sales department has asked for a credit limit of £20,000 for Oxford Ltd who is a potential new credit customer. Oxford Ltd has provided the following financial statements.

Summarised statements of profit or loss

	Year ending 31 December		
	20X8 £000	20X7 £000	20X6 £000
Sales revenue	2,660	2,570	2,520
Cost of sales	1,690	1,650	1,640
Gross profit	**970**	**920**	**880**
Operating expenses	580	540	510
Profit from operations	**390**	**380**	**370**
Finance costs (Interest payable)	90	80	75
Profit from operations before tax	**300**	**300**	**295**
Tax	72	76	72
Profit for the financial year	**228**	**224**	**223**

Summarised statements of financial position

	As at 31 December		
	20X8 £000	20X7 £000	20X6 £000
ASSETS			
Non-current assets	**3,741**	**3,380**	**3,029**
Current assets:			
Inventory	280	260	230
Trade receivables	550	540	510
Cash at bank	2	3	4
	832	**803**	**744**
Total assets	**4,573**	**4,183**	**3,773**
EQUITY AND LIABILITES			
Equity			
Ordinary share capital	800	800	800
Retained earnings	1,715	1,487	1,263

	As at 31 December		
	20X8 £000	20X7 £000	20X6 £000
Total equity	2,515	2,287	2,063
Non-current liabilities			
Borrowings (long-term loans)	1,600	1,400	1,200
Current liabilities			
Trade payables	370	380	395
Other payables	88	116	115
	458	496	510
Total liabilities	2,058	1,896	1,710
Total equity and liabilities	4,573	4,183	3,773

(a) (i) Calculate the key ratios for each of the three years for Oxford Ltd (to 2dp).

(ii) Rate the company using the credit rating (scoring) system.

	Indicator 20X8	Rating	Indicator 20X7	Rating	Indicator 20X6	Rating
Operating profit margin (%)						
Current ratio (:1)						
Accounts payable payment period (days)						
Gearing (%)						
Interest cover (times)						
Total						

(b) **Based on your results of your credit rating recommend whether the requested credit limit should be given to Oxford Ltd.**

Customer	Decision
Oxford Ltd	▼

Picklist:

Accept
Reject

· ·

Task 3

Communication and correspondence between the credit control function, customers and other parties is an important feature of having effective credit control system along with maintaining a good working relationships.

(a) **Prepare a note below outlining the methods of communications that can be used including factors to take into account when making these communications.**

Note

(b) Carmen Contractors Ltd is an existing customer and has been for many years. Carmen has requested that your company, FH Panels, extend Carmen's credit limit from £10,000 to £20,000. The company has provided its statements of profit or loss for each of the two years ended 31 March 20X5 and 20X6 and statements of financial position as at those dates.

Carmen Contractors Ltd: Statements of profit or loss for the years ending 31 March

	20X6 £000	20X5 £000
Revenue	5,600	5,000
Cost of sales	4,400	4,000
Gross profit	**1,200**	**1,000**
Operating expenses	850	800
Profit from operations	**350**	**200**
Finance costs	100	100
Profit from operations before tax	**250**	**100**
Taxation	80	20
Profit for the financial year	**170**	**80**

Carmen Contractors Ltd: Statements of financial position for year ending 31 March:

	20X6 £000	20X5 £000
ASSETS		
Non-current assets	**2,150**	**1,940**
Current assets		
Inventory	420	400
Trade receivables	220	140
	640	**540**
Total assets	**2,790**	**2,480**

	20X6 £000	20X5 £000
EQUITY AND LIABILITIES		
Equity		
Share capital	800	800
Retained earnings	380	210
Total equity	**1,180**	**1,010**
Current liabilities		
Trade payables	560	520
Overdraft	1,050	950
Total liabilities	**1,610**	**1,470**
Total equity and liabilities	**2,790**	**2,480**

Prepare a report for your supervisor analysing the results of Carmen Contractors for the last two years and concluding on whether the credit limit for the company should be extended as requested by Carmen.

Note

Task 4

You are the credit controller for Glenn Ltd and you have received a request for £30,000 of credit from a potential new customer, TG Ltd. TG Ltd has provided you with its latest set of financial statements which are summarised below:

Statements of profit or loss for the years ended 30 June

	20X9 £000	20X8 £000
Revenue	1,920	1,800
Cost of sales	1,490	1,400
Gross profit	**430**	**400**
Operating expenses	180	160
Profit from operations	**250**	**240**
Finance costs	56	38
Profit from operations before tax	**194**	**202**
Taxation	39	44
Profit for the financial year	**155**	**158**

Statements of financial position at 30 June

	20X9 £000	20X8 £000
ASSETS		
Non-current assets	**2,610**	**2,290**
Current assets		
Inventory	210	170
Trade receivables	270	280
	480	**450**
Total assets	**3,090**	**2,740**
EQUITY AND LIABILITIES		
Equity		
Share capital	1,200	1,200
Retained earnings	1,015	860

	20X9 £000	20X8 £000
Total equity	2,215	2,060
Current liabilities		
Trade payables	305	300
Bank overdraft	570	380
Total liabilities	875	680
Total equity and liabilities	3,090	2,740

Calculate the following financial ratios for TG Ltd to 2dp:

	20X9	20X8
Gross profit margin (%)		
Operating profit margin (%)		
Return on capital employed (%)		
Asset turnover		
Current ratio (:1)		
Quick ratio (:1)		
Inventory holding period (days)		
Accounts receivable collection period (days)		
Accounts payable payment period (days)		
Interest cover (times)		

Use the information from the previous pages to complete the following memo (using the picklists or by entering a number to the nearest whole number) assessing the financial statements of TG provided, reaching a conclusion as to the level of credit that should be extended to them.

Memo

Subject: Request for credit from TG Ltd

After the request from TG Ltd for £30,000 of credit I have examined the information that we have available about the company which includes the financial statements for the last two years.

Financial statements

The financial statements for TG Ltd for the last two years have been examined and the key ratios calculated under the headings of profitability, liquidity and gearing.

Although the company appears to be (1) [▼] there is some concern about the company's (2) [▼] . Both the current and quick ratios are (3) [▼] . The company appears to have been financed for the last two years by a (4) [▼] . The interest cover in 20X9 is (5) [▼] at over [ ] times.

The payables' payment period is [ ] days. Although it has (6) [▼] , it is (7) [▼] than the company's receivables' collection period. This could be (8) [▼] .

Conclusion

In the absence of any further information I suggest that we (9)

[▼]

Picklists – commentary on ratios:

(1) liquid
profitable

(2) liquidity
profitability

(3) seemingly very low and are decreasing
seemingly very high and are increasing
seemingly very low and are increasing
seeming very low and are decreasing

---

(4)   long-term loan
      substantial overdraft

(5)   reasonably healthy
      very unhealthy

(6)   risen by 4%
      fallen by 4%
      risen by 10%
      fallen by 10%

(7)   much longer
      much shorter

(8)   a sign the company's cash flow is improving
      a sign of overtrading

(9)   offer TG Ltd the £30,000 credit they have requested

      offer TG Ltd a trial period of credit at a lower level (eg £10,000) until
      further information is obtained

      refuse TG Ltd credit

Task 5

(a)   Which is the best description of a retention of title clause?

	✓
The purchaser has ownership of the goods when they are delivered	
The seller retains ownership of the goods until they are paid for	
The purchaser has ownership of the goods once the invoice is received	
The seller retains ownership of the goods until a cheque is put in the post	

(b) In the situation where an individual is declared bankrupt, the assets are distributed in a particular order.

Which of the following would receive assets first if assets of the bankrupt were distributed?

	✓
Preferential creditors	
The bankrupt	
Trade payables	
Secured creditors	

(c) **Which of the following statements are true or false regarding invoice discounting?**

	True	False
Invoice discounting is most associated with assisting businesses in their long term financing requirements		
Invoice discounting is where debts of a business are purchased at a discount to their face value		
Invoice discounting is a strategy of offering discounts to customers to encourage prompt payment		
When using invoice discounting the business often hands over control over their receivables ledger to the discounting agency		

(d) Complete the following statement.

There are a number of remedies to the injured party for a breach of contract.

When a court orders one party to the contract **not** to do something, then this remedy is commonly known as [▾].

Picklist:

an injunction
quantum meruit
specific performance
termination

(e) **Drag and drop the correct words into the following statement.**

A factoring service can help business with their [   ] term finance by advancing an agreed amount based on a business's outstanding trade [   ]

Factoring services can also offer [   ] against the risk of irrecoverable [   ]. The use of a factoring service is normally considered an [   ] method of credit management. A disadvantage of using this type of service is loss of customer [   ].

The drag and drop choices are:

debts
expensive
goods
goodwill
inexpensive
insurance
long
payables
receivables
short

(f) A business has proposed to increase the credit period that it gives to its customers from one month to two months in order to attract additional customers and increase sales revenue. The current figure for annual sales revenue is £576,000 and the product sells for £15 per unit. It is believed that the introduction of the new credit period will increase sales by an extra 3,600 units.

Calculate the existing value of receivables.

£ [   ]

Calculate the new value of receivables with increase of 3,600 units.

£ [   ]

Task 6

(a) A business currently trades on 30-day credit terms but is considering offering a settlement discount of 2% for payment within seven days of the invoice date.

Calculate the following to two decimal places.

The simple cost of the discount [   ] %

The compound annual cost of the discount [   ] %

(b) **In the absence of express statements as to whether or not legal relations are intended which of the following statements are true or false?**

	True	False
The courts always assume that legal relations were not intended		
The courts assume that legal relations were not intended unless they were social arrangements.		
The courts will assume that legal relations were intended unless the parties can prove otherwise		
The courts assume that legal relations were intended in commercial cases unless proved otherwise		

(c) A business offers its customers a 2% discount if they pay in the month of their purchase. Past experience has shown on average 75% of customers take up this offer with 15% paying the next month and the remaining 10% paying 2 months after their purchase date.

	January	February	March
Sales revenue	£47,000	£52,000	£50,000

Calculate the expected cash receipts in March.

£ [   ]

(d) **How is a credit limit for a new customer set?**

	✓
Based upon their payment of outstanding amounts in the past	
Based upon the amount that the customer wishes to purchase	
Based upon the risk assessment of the customer	
Based upon the recommendation of the sales representatives	

(e) A customer owing £32,000 to Jazdata Ltd has been declared bankrupt. Unsecured creditors are due to receive 15p in the pound from a final distribution to creditors.

Jazdata Ltd is a unsecured creditor and is not VAT registered.

Calculate the amount Jazdata Ltd should expect to receive from this distribution.

£

Calculate the amount Jazadata Ltd will write-off as an irrecoverable debt.

£

(f) **Which of the following statements are true or false?**

	True	False
Insolvency is where an individual cannot pay their debts		
Under an administrative order a customer must make regular agreed payments into court to pay off a debt.		
A liquidators job is to help ensure creditors receive payment		
In the event of a liquidation there is no strict order of distribution of assets		

Task 7

The debt collection policy and extract from the aged receivables' analysis and supporting customer notes are set out below.

Debt collection policy

Invoices must be sent out the day after the goods/service is provided.

All customers are required to pay within 30 days of the invoice date.

An aged receivables' analysis is produced monthly.

Statements are sent to all customers in the first week of each month.

When a debt is 7 days overdue a telephone call is made to the customer.

When a debt is 14 days overdue a reminder letter is sent to the customer.

If a debt becomes 30 days overdue the customer is put on the stop list and a meeting with the customer is arranged.

When a debt is 60 days overdue it is put into the hands of a debt collector.

When a debt is 90 days overdue legal proceedings are commenced subject to the agreement of the managing director.

Aged receivables' analysis at 30 June 20X9 – extract

Customer	Amount due £	Current £	31 to 60 days £	61 to 90 days £	> 90 days £
Havanna Ltd	11,250		11,250		
Jones Partners	8,000			8,000	
Norman Bros	11,100	10,700	400		
Kiera Ltd	23,000	12,000	10,000		1,000

Notes

- The outstanding invoice for Havanna Ltd is dated 20 May 20X9.
- The outstanding invoice for Jones Partners is dated 14 April 20X9.
- The invoices for Norman Bros were dated as follows:
    - £10,700 12 June 20X9
    - £400 17 May 20X9 – a telephone call was made on 28 June to chase this debt but there has been no response.
- The invoice to Kiera Ltd for £1,000 which is over 90 days old is in dispute as the customer claims that the goods were faulty and returned them. Kiera Ltd is a long-standing customer with a generally good record for paying although always takes longer than the 30 days credit period.

(a) **Review each of the four customers and complete the tables below discussing appropriate actions to take including whether any amounts should be provided for as doubtful or written-off as irrecoverable.**

Havanna Ltd

Jones Partners

Norman Bros

Kiera Ltd

Premier Electrics Ltd has suffered a power cut at their head office and have lost invoice information for August and September.

The following information is available from the aged receivables ledger:

Balance as at 1 August £27,500

Credit notes issued: 15 August £1,680 (including VAT), 8 September £800 net of VAT

Irrecoverable debts written-off: 26 September £460

Payments received: 20 August £62,720, 27 September £64,800

Balance as at 31 August £25,800

Balance as at 30 September £19,700

(b) **Calculate the sales invoice values for August and September.**

BPP PRACTICE ASSESSMENT 2
CREDIT MANAGEMENT

ANSWERS

Credit Management (CDMT)
BPP practice assessment 2

Task 1

(a)

	✓
The contract must be in writing	✓
The parties must be in agreement	
Each party must provide consideration	
Each party must intend legal relations	

(b) | An action for the goods | is a normal remedy for breach of contract due to non-payment of a debt.

(c)

	✓
Title, quantity, fitness	
Title, sale by sample, price	
Description, price, fitness	
Description, quality, fitness	✓

(d) Misrepresentation results in a contract being | voidable | .

(e)

	✓
(i) only	
(ii) only	
Both statements	
Neither statement	✓

Task 2

(a)

	Indicator 20X8	Rating	Indicator 20X7	Rating	Indicator 20X6	Rating
Operating profit margin (%)	14.66%	4	14.79%	4	14.68%	4
Current ratio (:1)	1.82	2	1.62	2	1.46	2
Accounts payable payment period (days)	79.91	–2	84.06	–2	87.91	–2
Gearing (%)	38.88	2	37.97	2	36.78	2
Interest cover (times)	4.33	4	4.75	4	4.93	4
Total		10		10		10

(b)

Customer	Decision
Oxford Ltd	Accept

Task 3

(a)

Note

Credit control communications can include the following:

Telephone

If a customer's account is overdue or if there is a dispute on the account these sometimes can be quickly and cheaply cleared up with a telephone call. When making a call it is important to keep the call professional and to make a note of date, reason for the call and if any action or outcome arose from the call. It is also good practice to record the name of the person spoken with for future reference. When calls are not answered or messages not responded to this can also give an indication of the credit status of a customer.

Statements

Statements should be sent to customers on a regular basis, for example monthly, and also when a particular debt is being pursued. The statement needs to contain all the relevant information including dates, invoices, credit notes and payments made. The statement may also include a remittance note to facilitate payment. Statements may be sent by post, sent by email or through secure online portals.

Chasing letters

A first chasing letter should be a gentle standardised reminder to encourage payment. At this stage the non-payment may be an oversight of the customer and a reminder letter may only be needed to obtain payment. If payment is not forthcoming then a firmer letter can be sent and may be composed on an individual basis and may be escalated to the chief credit controller for signing. This and subsequent chasing letters need to contain details of the amounts owing, the obligations of the customer to make payment and possible consequences of non-payment. Consequences can include having the account put on stop and possible legal action.

Solicitors and debt collection agencies

The credit control function will also need to instruct solicitors and debt collection agencies to take appropriate action. Communications here will be formal stating the facts of each specific situation. For speed and efficiency email is a popular form of communication between solicitors and other agencies. If email is used then these need to be saved for future evidence if need be.

(b)

To: Supervisor

From: Accounting Technician

Date:

Subject: Carmen Contractors Ltd – request for extension of credit limit

I have analysed the financial statements provided by Carmen Contractors Ltd for the years ending 31 March 20X5 and 20X6. The results of this analysis are set out below.

Profitability

Revenues have grown significantly during the year (by 12%). The gross profit margin has increased from 20% in 20X5 to 21.4% in 20X6. Both these increases have played a part in the increase in operating profit and the operating profit margin, increasing from 4% to 6.3%. Even though asset turnover has decreased slightly the significant increase in profit from operations has led to an impressive increase in return on capital employed (20X6: 29.7%, 20X5: 19.8%), increasing by almost 10%. The profitability indicators are therefore positive, however these need to be considered together with key liquidity indicators.

Liquidity

The company appears to operate with very low levels of liquidity with low figures for both the current ratio (0.4) and the quick ratio (0.1). This would appear to be largely due to very low levels of receivables and being financed by a large overdraft, which has increased by £100,000 during the year. The fact that the increased profits have not been converted to an improved cash position can probably be explained by the increased capital expenditure (non-current assets have increased by £210,000), and increasing inventory levels.

Of particular interest to us (as potential payables of the company) is their accounts payable payment period which has remained at around 46 to 47 days. As we offer only 30 days of credit then this is of some concern.

Interest cover

The business is heavily financed by a bank overdraft with the related interest charges. Interest cover was low in 20X5 at 2 times, but has improved in 20X6 to 3.5 times which is an encouraging sign, although this is due to improving profits since the overdraft itself increased and there was no fall in interest payable.

Summary and conclusion

Although profitability is improving, there are some causes for concern over the liquidity of the business. The revenue growth, taken together with the apparent capital expenditure, payables payment period and deteriorating cash position could be an indication Carmen is overtrading, and it would therefore be risky to increase the credit limit at this time.

The request to increase the credit limit to £20,000 should be refused until further investigation can be carried out.

Report appendix: summary of ratios

	20X6	20X5
Gross profit margin	21.4%	20.0%
Operating profit margin	6.3%	4.0%
Return on capital employed	29.7%	19.8%
Asset turnover	4.75	4.95
Current ratio	0.4 : 1	0.4 : 1
Quick (acid test) ratio	0.1 : 1	0.1 : 1
Inventory holding period	35 days	37 days
Accounts receivable collection period	14 days	10 days
Accounts payable payment period	46 days	47 days
Interest cover	3.5 times	2.0 times

Task 4

	20X9	20X8
Gross profit margin (%)	22.40	22.22
Operating profit margin (%)	13.02	13.33
Return on capital employed (%)	11.29	11.65
Asset turnover	0.87	0.87
Current ratio (:1)	0.55	0.66
Quick ratio (:1)	0.31	0.41

	20X9	20X8
Inventory holding period (days)	51.44	44.32
Accounts receivable collection period (days)	51.33	56.78
Accounts payable payment period (days)	74.71	78.21
Interest cover (times)	4.46	6.32

Memo

Subject: Request for credit from TG Ltd

After the request from TG Ltd for £30,000 of credit I have examined the information that we have available about the company which includes the financial statements for the last two years.

Financial statements

The financial statements for TG Ltd for the last two years have been examined and the key ratios calculated under the headings of profitability, liquidity and gearing.

Although the company appears to be [profitable] there is some concern about the company's [liquidity]. Both the current and quick ratios are [seemingly very low and are decreasing]. The company appears to have been financed for the last two years by a [substantial overdraft]. The interest cover is [reasonably healthy] at over [4] times.

The payables' payment period is [75] days. Although it has [fallen by 4%], it is [much longer] than the company's receivables' collection period. This could be [a sign of overtrading].

Conclusion

In the absence of any further information I suggest that we

[offer TG Ltd a trial period of credit at a lower level (eg £10,000) until further] [is obtained].

Task 5

(a)

	✓
The purchaser has ownership of the goods when they are delivered	
The seller retains ownership of the goods until they are paid for	✓
The purchaser has ownership of the goods once the invoice is received	
The seller retains ownership of the goods until a cheque is put in the post	

(b)

	✓
Preferential creditors	
The bankrupt	
Trade payables	
Secured creditors	✓

(c)

	True	False
Invoice discounting is most associated with assisting businesses in their long term financing requirements		✓
Invoice discounting is where debts of a business are purchased at a discount to their face value	✓	
Invoice discounting is a strategy of offering discounts to customers to encourage prompt payment		✓
When using invoice discounting the business often hands over control over their receivables ledger to the discounting agency		✓

(d) There are a number of remedies to the injured party for a breach of contract.

When a court orders one party to the contract **not** to do something, then this remedy is commonly known as an injunction .

(e) A factoring service can help business with their short term finance by advancing an agreed amount based on a business's outstanding trade receivables .

Factoring services can also offer insurance against the risk of irrecoverable debts . The use of a factoring service is normally considered an expensive method of credit management. A disadvantage of using this type of service is loss of customer goodwill .

(f) The existing value of receivables is:

£ | 48,000

The new value of receivables with increase of 3,600 units is:

£ | 105,000

Task 6

(a) The simple cost of the discount | 32.39 | %

The compound annual cost of the discount | 37.80 | %

(b)

	True	False
The courts always assume that legal relations were not intended		✓
The courts assume that legal relations were not intended unless they were social arrangements.		✓
The courts will assume that legal relations were intended unless the parties can prove otherwise		✓
The courts assume that legal relations were intended in commercial cases unless proved otherwise	✓	

(c) The expected cash receipts in March amount to:

£	49,250

(d)

	✓
Based upon their payment of outstanding amounts in the past	
Based upon the amount that the customer wishes to purchase	
Based upon the risk assessment of the customer	✓
Based upon the recommendation of the sales representatives	

(e) The amount Jazdata Ltd should expect to receive from this distribution is:

£	4,800

The amount Jazadata Ltd will write-off as an irrecoverable debt is:

£	27,200

(f)

	True	False
Insolvency is where an individual cannot pay their debts		✓
Under an administrative order a customer must make regular agreed payments into court to pay off a debt.	✓	
A liquidators job is to help ensure creditors receive payment	✓	
In the event of a liquidation there is no strict order of distribution of assets		✓

Task 7

(a) Havanna Ltd

This debt is now 11 days overdue and a telephone call should be made to the customer. It should be pointed out that the debt for £11,250 is now overdue and it should be established whether there is any query with regard to the debt. If there is no query then a date for payment should be established. If there is a problem with this amount then consideration should be given to making an allowance.

Jones Partners

This debt is now more than 30 days overdue and therefore the customer should be put on the stop list and no further credit sales made to this customer. A meeting with the customer should also be arranged in order to establish when the amount of £8,000 is to be paid. An allowance for this amount should probably be made.

Norman Bros

The debt of £10,700 is not yet overdue but the debt for £400 is 14 days overdue and there has been no response to the telephone call made on 28 June. Therefore a strongly but courteously worded reminder letter should be sent to the customer stating the amount that is overdue of £400 and that payment should be sent within seven days or further action will be taken.

Kiera Ltd

It would appear that the dispute with Kiera Ltd is genuine but this must be checked with a telephone call and checking the records of returned goods. If this amount is a genuine dispute then it will probably need to be written off as an irrecoverable debt given the customer's record of paying in the past.

(b)

August		September	
1 August balance:	(£27,500)	1 September balance b/f:	(£25,800)
Credit notes issued:	£1,680	Credit notes issued (inc VAT)	£960
Payments received:	£62,720	Payments received	£64,800
		Debts written-off	£460
31 August c/f	£25,800	30 September balance	£19,700
Sales (bal fig)	**£62,700**	**Sales (bal fig)**	**£60,120**

BPP PRACTICE ASSESSMENT 3
CREDIT MANAGEMENT

Time allowed: 2 hours and 30 minutes

Credit Management (CDMT)
BPP practice assessment 3

Task 1

(a)   Complete the following sentences about The Late Payment of Commercial Debts (Interest) Act 1998.

The Late Payment of Commercial Debts (Interest) Act 1998 entitles a business selling goods to charge statutory interest. This can be charged to the buyer

starting from [   ]. Statutory

interest is made up of the Bank of England base rate plus [   ] %. The

interest chargeable applies to [▼].

A compensation entitlement can be charged [▼].

Picklist:

as well as interest
instead of interest
the 21st day after the sale took place
the day after the agreed date for payment
the day the order was received
the day the sale took place
the specific overdue debt excluding VAT
the specific overdue debt including VAT
the total amount owed by the customer

(b)   Drag and drop the correct words into the following statement.

Care must be taken to distinguish between an offer and an invitation to treat. An invitation to treat is an [   ] by the [   ] of the goods for the [   ] to make an offer to [   ] them at that price.

Picklist:

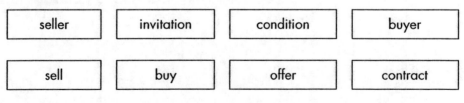

| seller | invitation | condition | buyer |
| sell | buy | offer | contract |

(c) Match each type of remedy for breach of contract on the left to the appropriate definition on the right by clicking on the left box first then on the corresponding right box. You can remove a line by clicking on it

Remedy	Definition
Injunction	A court order that one of the parties must fulfill its obligations
	Compensation for loss
Termination	Payment ordered for the part of the contract performed
	One party refusing to carry on with the contract
Quantum meruit	One party to the contract being ordered by the court not to do something

Karen attended a presentation by a beauty products supplier where she ordered 500 different beauty products. The layout in the room was intimidating and employees of the beauty products supplier blocked the exits forcing those attending to place orders. After she had left, Karen learned that she could void the contract.

(d) **The contract between Karen and the beauty products supplier is voidable due to:**

	✓
Mistake	
Fraud	
Coercion	
Consumer Credit	

(e) **Identify whether the following statements contract law are true or false.**

Consideration does not have to be in the form of goods or money. [▼]

Contracts can be voidable due to coercion where one party to the contract uses threatening behaviour towards the other party. [▼]

Consideration can be a promise to do something in the future. [▼]

Picklist:

False

True

::

Task 2

Scootlike plc uses a credit rating system to assess the credit status of new customers.

The credit rating (scoring) system below is used to assess the risk of default by calculating key indicators (ratios), comparing them to the table and calculating an aggregate score.

Credit rating (scoring) system	Score
Operating profit margin	–5
Losses	0
Less than 5%	5
5% and above but less than 10%	10
10% and above but less than 20%	20
20% or more	
Interest cover	
No cover	–30
Less than 1	–20
1 and above but less than 2	–10
2 and above but less than 4	0
4 or more	10
Current ratio	
Less than 1	–20
1 and above but less than 1.25	–10
1.25 and above but less than 1.5	0
1.5 or more	10
Gearing (total debt/total debt plus equity)	
Less than 25%	20
25% and above but less than 50%	10
50% and above but less than 65%	0
65% and above but less than 75%	–20
75% and above but less than 80%	–40
80% or more	–100

Risk	Aggregate score
Very low risk	Between 60 and 21
Low risk	Between 20 and 1
Medium risk	Between 0 and –24
High risk	Between –25 and –50
Very high risk	Between –51 and –160

The Sales department has asked for a credit limit of £50,000 to be given to Wallace Ltd, a potential new customer. The financial information below has been supplied by Wallace Ltd.

Wallace Ltd statement of profit or loss	20X5 £000	20X4 £000
Sales revenue	9,875	7,324
Cost of sales	7,450	5,800
Gross profit	**2,425**	**1,524**
Distribution costs	1,000	900
Administration expenses	900	900
Operating profit/(loss)	**525**	**(276)**
Finance costs	200	100
Profit/(loss) before taxation	**325**	**(376)**
Taxation	65	0
Profit/(loss) for the year	**260**	**(376)**

Wallace Ltd statement of financial position	20X5 £000	20X4 £000
Assets		
Non-current assets		
Property, plant and equipment	3,700	2,500
Current assets		
Inventories	400	450
Trade and other receivables	200	180
Cash	5	10
	605	640
Total assets	4,305	3,140
Equity and liabilities		
Equity		
Share capital	1,500	1,500
Retained earnings	510	250
Total equity	2,010	1,750
Non-current liabilities		
Borrowing	2,000	1,000
Current liabilities		
Borrowing	100	0
Trade and other payables	195	390
Total liabilities	2,295	1,390
Total equity and liabilities	4,305	3,140

(a) **Complete the table below by calculating the key indicators (to two decimal places) for 20X5 and 20X4 for Wallace Ltd, and rate the company using the credit rating scoring system.**

Wallace Ltd	20X5 Indicator	20X5 Rating	20X4 Indicator	20X4 Rating
Operating profit margin %				
Interest cover				
Current ratio				
Gearing %				
Total credit rating				

Rating	Decision
Very low or low risk current year and very low or low risk previous year	Accept
Very low or low risk current year and medium risk previous year	Accept
Very low or low risk current year and high or very high risk previous year	Request latest management accounts and defer decision
Very high risk or high risk current year	Reject
Medium risk current year and medium, low or very low risk previous year	Accept
Medium risk current year and high or very high risk previous year	Request latest management accounts and defer decision

(b) **Based on the results of your credit rating and using the table above, recommend whether the requested credit limit should be given to Wallace Ltd.**

Customer	Decision
Wallace Ltd	▼

Picklist:

Accept

Reject

Request latest management accounts and defer decision

Task 3

Lomond Ltd is a manufacture of outdoor clothing. Ben Ltd is a potential new customer and has approached Lomond Ltd to ask for a credit limit of £1,500.

Lomond Ltd has standard terms of trade of 30 days.

The sales director has advised you that she has invited the directors of Ben Ltd to a spa day next month, as she is keen to gain Ben's business. The sales director receives a bonus based on the amount of new business she brings in.

Lomond Ltd employs an Accounts Receivables Clerk. She records all credit sales and all payments by customers. She also prints an aged receivables analysis every Monday morning and gives it to the Finance Manager. There is no Credit Controller. The Finance Manager would like the accounts receivables clerk to carry out additional tasks that would reduce the risk of Lomond having to write off more bad debts.

(a) **Write notes to brief a new member of the credit control team explaining three sources of external information you will use (other than financial statements) when assessing whether to grant credit to a new customer. Comment on the role of the sales director in the credit assessment process.**

(b) **Write notes to brief the Accounts Receivable Clerk to identify three tasks that the clerk could carry out that would reduce the risk of Lomond having to write off more bad debts. Explain how each task would help to reduce the risk.**

Ben has supplied the following information based on the last two years of trading.

Ben Limited Statement of financial position	20X5 £	20X4 £
Assets		
Non-current assets		
Property, plant and equipment	8,544	7,800
Current assets		
Inventories	600	900
Trade and other receivables	1,800	1,800
Cash	10	10
	2,410	2,710
Total assets	**10,954**	**10,510**

Ben Limited Statement of financial position	20X5 £	20X4 £
Equity and liabilities		
Equity		
Share capital	2,500	2,500
Retained earnings	2,754	1,330
Total equity	**5,254**	**3,830**
Non-current liabilities		
Borrowing	3,000	2,500
Current liabilities		
Trade and other payables	2,000	2,100
Taxation	200	180
Borrowing	500	1,900
	2,700	**4,180**
Total liabilities	**5,700**	**6,680**
Total equity and liabilities	**10,954**	**10,510**

Ben Limited Statement of profit or loss	20X5 £	20X4 £
Sales revenue	30,000	28,000
Cost of sales	24,020	21,830
Gross profit	**5,980**	**6,170**
Distribution costs	2,400	2,000
Administration expenses	1,300	1,300
Operating profit	**2,280**	**2,870**
Finance costs	500	600
Profit before taxation	**1,780**	**2,270**
Taxation	356	454
Profit for the year	**1,424**	**1,816**

Ben Limited	20X5	20X4
Gross profit margin %	19.93	22.03
Operating profit margin %	7.60	10.25
Interest cover	4.56	4.78
Current ratio	0.89	0.65
Trade payables payment period in days	30	35
Trade receivables collection period in days	22	23
Inventory holding period in days	9	15
Gearing %	40	53

The following additional information has also been provided.

1. Ben Ltd operates as an outdoor clothing retailer. It is planning to expand by acquiring more retail outlets. This is attractive to Lomond Ltd as it will mean they will buy more clothing to stock the new stores.

2. Ben Ltd has approached its bank to request additional borrowings to finance the acquisition of the new stores. It is expecting to find out within the next couple of weeks if the request has been approved. They have submitted a request to borrow an additional £3,000 repayable over 10 years.

3. During 20X5 Ben changed the mix of clothing stocked in each of its stores. It has increased the number of lower priced products as demand for these products is high from customers.

4. Lomond Ltd generally buys its own supplies on short credit terms. For that reason the company is reluctant to agree terms longer than 30 days to any customer. The 30 day terms are 30 days after the month when the sale took place.

(c) In your capacity as a member of the Finance Team, write a note to the Finance Manager analysing the information. You should recommend whether credit should be granted to Ben Ltd.

Task 4

The Sales department of Lightup Ltd has asked for a credit limit of £75,000 to be given to Glow Limited who is a potential new customer. The financial information below has been supplied by Glow Limited in respect of the last two years. Lightup Ltd trades on 30 day terms.

Glow Limited Statement of profit or loss	20X5 £000	20X4 £000
Sales revenue	20,500	23,200
Cost of sales	8,900	7,900
Gross profit	**11,600**	**15,300**
Distribution costs	8,000	7,000
Administration expenses	4,500	4,300
Operating profit/(loss)	**(900)**	**4,000**
Finance costs	500	550
Profit/(loss) before taxation	**(1,400)**	**3,450**
Taxation	0	690
Profit/(loss) for the year	**(1,400)**	**2,760**

Glow Limited Statement of financial position	20X5 £000	20X4 £000
Assets		
Non-current asses		
Properly, plant and equipment	23,900	20,500
Current assets		
Inventories	4,250	3,989
Trade and other receivables	4,901	5,072
Cash	4,300	5,525
	13,451	14,586
Total assets	**37,351**	**35,086**

Glow Limited Statement of financial position	20X5 £000	20X4 £000
Equity and liabilities		
Equity		
Share capital	4,100	3,950
Retained earnings	5,615	7,015
Total equity	**9,715**	**10,965**
Non-current liabilities		
Borrowing	21,500	19,800
Current liabilities		
Borrowing	2,750	2,590
Trade and other payables	3,386	1,731
Total liabilities	**27,636**	**24,121**
Total equity and liabilities	**37,351**	**35,086**

Complete the email to the Chief Credit Controller, calculating and commenting on key ratios and conclude by recommending whether or not credit should be extended. All calculations should be given to two decimal places.

Email

To: Credit Controller   **Date:**   Today

From: AAT Technician   **Subject:**   New Customer Glow Ltd

Please find below my calculations. observations and recommendation for new customer Glow Ltd.

Profitability

The sales revenue has decreased [   ] % which may be a bad sign. The gross profit margin has reduced from [   ] % in 20X4 to [   ] % in 20X5. This means that [⮟].

The gross profit has fallen in absolute terms by [   ]%. The most important indicator of profitability is the operating profit margin which has fallen from [   ] % in 20X4 to [   ] % in 20X5.

The operating loss has been caused by a combination of the [☑] in gross profit and the increase of [   ] % in combined distribution and administration costs.

Picklist:

decrease
increase
the selling price and cost of sales have decreased.
the selling price and cost of sales have increased.
the selling price has decreased or the cost of sales has increased.
the selling price has increased or the cost of sales has decreased.

Liquidity

The current ratio has fallen from [   ] in 20X4 to [   ] in 20X5. This is because there has been an increase in current liabilities and [☑] in current assets. The business still has cash in hand, although this has fallen by [   ] %. The inventory holding period has [☑] from [   ] days in 20X4 to [   ] days in 20X5.

The trade receivables collection period has [☑] from [   ] days in 20X4 to [   ] days in 20X5. The payables payment period has increased from [   ] days in 20X4 to [   ] days in 20X5.

Picklist:

a decrease
an increase
improved from
worsened from

Gearing

Both long-term and short-term borrowing have increased. The gearing ratio (debt/debt + equity) has increased to [   ] % in 20X5. This may have been as a result of acquiring new plant and equipment.

Recommendation

I recommend that [☑].

Picklist:

we defer the decision and ask for further information about future plans
we grant the credit limit as requested
we refuse the credit limit as requested

Task 5

(a) **Match each type of claim on the left to the appropriate type of court procedure on the right by clicking on the left box first then on the corresponding right box. You can remove a line by clicking on it**

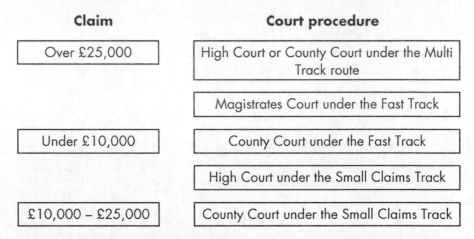

Claim	Court procedure
Over £25,000	High Court or County Court under the Multi Track route
	Magistrates Court under the Fast Track
Under £10,000	County Court under the Fast Track
	High Court under the Small Claims Track
£10,000 – £25,000	County Court under the Small Claims Track

(b) **Which of the following statements are true in the context of bankruptcy and insolvency?**

	True ✓	False ✓
Bankruptcy arises where an individual cannot pay his or her debts and is declared bankrupt.		
Insolvency is where a company cannot pay its debts as they fall due.		
If a trade receivable owes an amount of at least £10,000 a statutory demand can be issued for payment of the amount due within a certain period of time		
A statutory demand should be made within four months of the debt. If the debt is older than four months a court has to be contacted to explain the reasons behind the delay.		

XYZ Ltd is considering alternative ways of managing debt collection. XYZs total receivables ledger balance as at 31 December 20X5 is £3,100,000, which includes £150,000 of debts which are over 90 days.

WRW Co can provide XYZ with a facility whereby WRW manages the receivables ledger on behalf of XYZ. WRW will lend XYZ a maximum of £1,800,000 or 70% of the outstanding receivables balance excluding debts over 90 days. WRW will not provide any protection against irrecoverable debts.

(c) **Complete the following sentences.**

WRW is offering [🔽] .

XYZ can borrow: [£ |]

Picklist:

a non-recourse factoring facility
a non-recourse invoice discounting facility
a recourse factoring facility
a recourse invoice discounting facility

(d) **Which of the following are key necessities for goods under the Consumer Rights Act?**

(i)   Of satisfactory quality
(ii)   At a reasonable price
(iii)   Fit for purpose
(iv)   As described

	✓
(i), (iii) and (iv)	
(i) and (iii)	
All of the above	
(ii) and (iv)	

(e) **Drag and drop the correct words into the following statement.**

Conditions and warranties are two types of terms within a contact. If one party breaks either of them, the other party can sue for [   ]. If one party breaks a [   ] the other party can choose to void the contract.

Picklist:

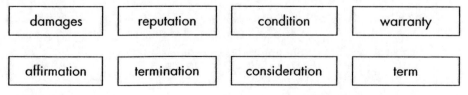

damages	reputation	condition	warranty
affirmation	termination	consideration	term

(f) **Which of the following is the correct definition of a garnishee order?**

	✓
An order issued by a High Court entitling the creditor to instruct an agent to collect assets from the debtor.	
An order issued by a court entitling the creditor to enter the premises of the debtor to seize assets to the value of the debt.	
An order issued by a County Court entitling the creditor to instruct a court employee to collect assets from the debtor	
An order issued by a court entitling a credit to collect payment from the customer of their debtor.	

Task 6

The Sales Manager of Hertogenbosch has found that her sales staff do not understand the annual percentage cost of the early settlement discounts that the company offers to customers.

(a) **Complete the following email.**

Email

To: Sales Staff   **Date:** Today

From: AAT Technician   **Subject:** Early Settlement Discounts

Please find below my explanation of how an annual percentage cost of an early settlement discount is calculated.

The effective rate of interest

If a customer pays promptly to take advantage of a 1% early settlement discount, we will receive 99% of the invoice total. This means that the discount we are giving the customer is ☐▾ of the amount they pay us. This is what it costs us to receive the cash earlier than our normal credit terms. It is called the effective rate of interest.

Discount periods

If the normal credit terms require customers to pay within 30 days of receiving an invoice, and the discount applies if the customer pays within 14 days, we are offering the discount in return for paying 16 days earlier than our normal terms. There are ☐▾ discount periods of 16 days in a 365 day year.

Annual percentage cost of the early settlement discount using simple interest rates

The annual percentage cost is found by [▾] the effective rate of interest and the discount periods in a year. The annual percentage cost of offering 1% discount to customers paying within 14 days rather than 30 days is [▾] to the nearest whole percent. I trust this will help you in any discussions with customers about early settlement discounts.

AAT Technician

Picklist:

adding
multiplying
square rooting
1%
1.01%
98.99%
99%
100%
12.17
22.81
26.07
29
23
23.82

Lexi Ltd wishes to offer a 2% discount to its customers for settlement of invoices within 21 days.

Lexi's Ltd's standard terms of trade are 45 days.

(b)   Calculate the compound annual cost of each discount to two decimal places.

The simple annual cost of the discount is [   ] %.

The compound annual cost of the discount is [   ] %.

(c) **Which of the following will deteriorate the liquidity of a business?**

	✓
Allowing customers extended credit terms to encourage them to buy more.	
Requiring a deposit with orders and settlement upon delivery of goods.	
Paying suppliers after their required date and forfeiting a settlement discount.	
Moving production to a just in time inventory system	

Austin's customers currently pay 30 days after the month end. He is introducing a 1% discount from month 2 if customers settle the invoice in the same month. It is expected that 80% of customers will take advantage of this. The expected sales revenue per month is as follows:

	Sales revenue
Month 1	£100,000
Month 2	£115,000
Month 3	£155,000

(d) **Calculate expected cash receipts in month 3.**

£	

(e) **Which of the following statements are true in order for Dunit to be able to successfully reclaim VAT on an unpaid debt?**

	✓
The debt must have remained unpaid for four months after the due date.	
Dunit must have made a provision for the unpaid debt	
The claim must be made within three years of the due date of payment of the debt.	
Dunit must already have accounted for the VAT and paid it over to HMRC	

Graham has received a letter from the liquidator of John Ltd. The liquidator has indicated that all unsecured creditors of John will receive a dividend of 4.5p in the pound (£) later in the year. Graham is owed £20,000 by John.

(f) **Calculate the amount that Patrick should write off as an irrecoverable debt. Ignore VAT. Show your answer to the nearest penny.**

Task 7

Onegym Ltd manufactures, supplies and assembles gym equipment. It also manufactures sports equipment that is custom made to specific customer requirements. VAT is charged at the standard rate on all supplies.

Onegym includes an all monies retention of title clause as part of its standard terms of trade. Equipment that is custom made to a specific customer order carries a unique serial number for warranty purposes. Payment terms are 30 days from the invoice date.

Onegym has credit insurance for certain named customer accounts.

You work in the credit control department of Onegym. Your supervisor is away on holiday and is not contactable, however you have been provided with the information below. Today's date is 31 December.

(a) **Review the information provided for each customer below and prepare comments and an action plan for dealing with the outstanding amounts due to Onegym. Your action plan should include a summary of the options available to Onegym to pursue outstanding amounts, along with recommendations for provisions or write off of irrecoverable debts where appropriate.**

PYL

PYL is a regular customer of Onegym and always pays to terms. PYL had ordered 12 custom-built treadmills for use in a new high altitude training tent. The order had specified that all 12 treadmills to be delivered by 15 October in time for the project to begin. Onegym delivered six computers on 14 October. However, due to the extended absence of their engineer Onegym could only deliver the remaining six computers on 29 October.

The total value of the invoice to PYL dated 30 October is £72,000 including VAT. PYL has complained about the late delivery, stating that this has significantly delayed their important project. They are withholding payment and asking for compensation. PYL account for approximately 20% of Onegym's total revenue.

DUU

Onegym has received notification that DUU is in receivership. The amount of the outstanding debt is £35,000 including VAT. The receiver has told Onegym that they will not accept any retention of title claim as the goods in question are generic items of small gym equipment such as hand weights that DUU has purchased from a number of different suppliers. It will therefore not be possible to identify which had been supplied by Onegym.

The account is credit insured for a maximum of 75% of the net debt or £20,000, whichever is the lower.

JCC

JCC has an outstanding invoice for £10,000, including VAT. The invoice is dated 1 September. JCC has often been slow to pay in the past, and has now given several excuses to delay payment, ranging from being unable to trace any of the original documentation to the authorised cheque signatory being away on holiday. Onegym has supplied JCC with copies of all relevant documentation and, in accordance with the credit control policy, is now about to instruct a debt collection agency or commence legal action.

The HR director has asked you to refrain from sending the debt collectors or instructing solicitors because the Managing Director of JCC is president of the local running club. She wishes to join this club, and she is concerned that any unpleasant tension will affect her application.

Onegym has had some problems with certain customer accounts following a manufacturing error in their popular cross trainer. The accounts department has managed to recover the following details relating to the account of ULK:

- Balance at 1 November: £60,000 (debit)

- Invoices raised: 5 November £22,000 net of VAT, 12 November £15,000 including VAT

- Credit notes issued: 16 November £3,500 including VAT, 14 December £3,100 including VAT

- Late payment charge processed in November relating to an overdue invoice from June: £300

- Balance at 31 November: £52,800 (debit)

- Balance at 31 December: £1,200 (credit)

(b) **Calculate the payments received from ULK in November and in December.**

BPP PRACTICE ASSESSMENT 3
CREDIT MANAGEMENT

ANSWERS

Credit Management (CDMT)
BPP practice assessment 3

Task 1

(a) Complete the following sentences about The Late Payment of Commercial Debts (Interest) Act 1998.

The Late Payment of Commercial Debts (Interest) Act 1998 entitles a business selling goods to charge statutory interest. This can be charged to the buyer starting from | the day after the agreed date for payment |. Statutory interest is made up of the Bank of England base rate plus | 8 | %. The interest chargeable applies to | the specific overdue debt including VAT |. A compensation entitlement can be charged | as well as interest |.

(b) Drag and drop the correct words into the following statement.

Care must be taken to distinguish between an offer and an invitation to treat. An invitation to treat is an | invitation | by the | seller | of the goods for the | buyer | to make an offer to | buy | them at that price.

(c) Match each type of remedy for breach of contract on the left to the appropriate definition on the right by clicking on the left box first then on the corresponding right box. You can remove a line by clicking on it

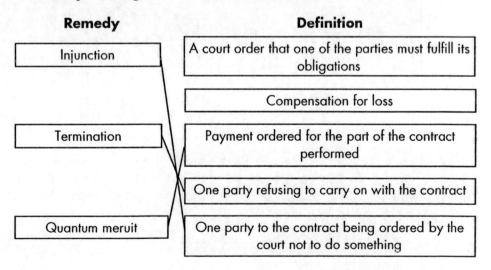

Remedy	Definition
Injunction	A court order that one of the parties must fulfill its obligations
	Compensation for loss
Termination	Payment ordered for the part of the contract performed
	One party refusing to carry on with the contract
Quantum meruit	One party to the contract being ordered by the court not to do something

(d) **The contract between Karen and the beauty retailer is voidable due to:**

	✓
Mistake	
Fraud	
Coercion	✓
Consumer Credit	

(e) **Identify whether the following statements about contract law are true or false.**

Consideration does not have to be in the form of goods or money.

| True |

Contracts can be voidable due to coercion where one party to the contract uses threatening behaviour towards the other party. | True |

Consideration cannot be a promise to do something in the future.

| False |

Task 2

(a) **Complete the table below by calculating the key indicators (to two decimal places) for 20X5 and 20X4 for Wallace Ltd, and rate the company using the credit rating scoring system.**

Wallace Ltd	20X5 Indicator	20X5 Rating	20X4 Indicator	20X4 Rating
Operating profit margin %	5.32	10	–3.77	–5
Interest cover	2.63	0	–2.76	–30
Current ratio	2.05	10	1.64	10
Gearing %	51.09	0	36.36	10
Total credit rating		20		–15

(b) **Based on the results of your credit rating and using the table above, recommend whether the requested credit limit should be given to Wallace Ltd.**

Customer	Decision	
Wallace Ltd	Accept	▼

Task 3

(a) **Write notes to brief a new member of the credit control team explaining three sources of external information you will use (other than financial statements) when assessing whether to grant credit to a new customer. Comment on the role of the sales director in the credit assessment process.**

There are a wide variety of sources which can be used when assessing the granting of credit, both internal and external. We will usually try to use a combination of sources in order to try to get the fullest picture of whether a new customer is an acceptable credit risk.

External sources of information include bank references, trade references, credit rating agencies, credit circles, and industry/trade publications. Bank references must be interpreted carefully, as banks have a duty of confidentiality. Their first regard is to their own customer and references are therefore usually worded in fairly standard ways – and we must try to interpret the 'real' meaning behind this. Banks will only give an opinion on the overall soundness of the customer and will not be able to tell us how quickly they might pay their debts.

Trade references are responses from other companies who have dealt with the prospective customer and may be able to tell us something about their payment profile. However, it is important to bear in mind that the customer has nominated these references and may have selected only those who might reply favourably.

Credit rating/reference agencies are organisations who maintain databases of information about individuals and businesses. The amount of information can be detailed (eg payment history, bankruptcy proceedings, court judgements etc) but can be out of date.

Credit Circles are groups of businesses in the same type of industry who have customers in common with each other and who meet on a regular basis. The sharing of information (often on an informal basis) can give useful and timely information on any possible problems with customers.

Trade publications and the media can sometimes be useful when considering the type of business a potential customer is in, and can help to see what overall trade views are on specific businesses, although it is important to check the facts behind any opinions provided in articles.

The sales director should have minimal input when assessing whether to grant credit. Whilst she may be knowledgeable about the industry, her role is to increase sales and undertake marketing activities and she may not be knowledgeable about the process of credit control and the importance of liquidity and credit management.

In any event, the sales director's role is primarily sales driven, and she may be influenced by the fact that she receives a bonus based on the amount of new business.

(b)

1. Follow a procedure when invoices have not been settled within the credit terms.

   A telephone call or a letter notifying a client that the date due has passed is likely to lead to payment more quickly than ignoring it.

   The procedure will give the clerk a date on which an overdue account should be passed to a debt collection agency or when to initiate court action. This is easier than leaving the decision of when to initiate action to the clerk.

2. Notifying the Finance Manager of any reasons offered by customers for non-payment

   Any claims that goods supplied were not satisfactory can be addressed quickly so that no reason remains for late or non-payment of an invoice.

3. Notifying the sales representatives

   This can enable the sales representatives to make personal contact with the firm and remind them of their obligation to pay on time.

4. Keeping records of credit checks carried out on new credit customers

   These can be used to compare with the actual payment records from the customers, and enable prompt responses to any not keeping to terms.

(c)

Profitability

- The sales revenue has increased by 7%. This could be due to the change in product mix and meeting customer demand by stocking more lower priced products. Ben is looking to expand and therefore revenue is expected to grow in 20X6, this is likely to lead to growth for ourselves if they increase their purchases from us.

- The gross margin has fallen slightly as a percentage.

- This has resulted in a fall in gross profit is £190 compared to last year as an absolute amount.

- The operating profit margin has fallen by 2.6%.

- Operating profit in absolute values is £590 lower.

This fall in gross profitability as a % may have been caused by:

- Change in product mix
- Selling more lower priced goods which will generate a lower margin

The fall in the operating profit value can be attributed to an increase in distribution costs:

- Distribution costs rose by 20%. Ben will need to investigate what has caused this increase and look to reduce distribution costs as it is eroding their operating profit.

- Interest cover is 4.56 compared to 4.78 times last year. The fall is due to a reduction in interest cost. Despite an increase of £500 in long term borrowings in 20X5, the interest cost has fallen due to a reduction in short term borrowing of £1,400 which are likely to have incurred a higher percentage rate of interest. Ben has a comfortable interest cover indication that it is able to take on more debt.

Liquidity

- The current ratio is higher than the previous year meaning liquidity appears to have improved. The fact that it is below 1 is not concerning as this is often the case for a retail company.

- The receivables collection period has reduced from 23 to 22 days which is good and indicates that Ben is efficient at collecting payment from its customers whom they sell to on credit.

- The cash balance is low for both years; however, this is to be expected given that it appears that Ben have been using their cash generated from operations to repay their borrowings.

- Inventory also appears to be being managed adequately as the holding period has fallen from 15 to 9 days.

- As the sales revenue has increased, reducing the inventory holding days indicates improved inventory management.

- The trade payables payment period has fallen from 35 to 30 days. This is an improvement. It might reflect a change to the terms of trade they have with suppliers. It is also comforting to us that they are able to pay within the 30 days terms that we would expect if we accepted them as a credit customer.
- Working capital appears to have been managed relatively efficiently.

Gearing and risk

- The gearing has decreased from 53% to 40%. This is reassuring in terms of Ben's current debt.
- The level of short-term borrowing has reduced by £1,400. This is a good sign.
- However, the company is planning expansion. If the company is successful in securing new borrowing from their bank to acquire new retail sites the level of gearing will rise.
- In terms of gearing there is little financial risk as gearing has reduced and interest cover is comfortable.
- Business risk. The business appears growing and expanding. Expansion into new locations may bring with it some risk. The business appears to be well managed and able to generate profits and cash.

Conclusion/Recommendation

- The performance indicators seem acceptable. The business is making a profit and managing its working capital well.
- Our standard terms are 30 days. Ben's financial statements show they are able to settle their current credit accounts within these terms.
- The amount of credit requested is £1,500. This is lower than their total trade payables at the end of 20X5.
- As a total amount of credit, £1,500 for a £30,000 turnover business is looks acceptable.
- Whether Ben expands and receives the increased borrowing facility from its bank or not would not be critical to the decision to grant additional credit.
- I recommend that we grant the credit limit of £1,500.
- If credit is to be granted, further comfort in the way of retention of title clauses, credit insurance or directors' guarantees might be considered.

Task 4

Complete the email to the Chief Credit Controller, calculating and commenting on key ratios and conclude by recommending whether or not credit should be extended. All calculations should be given to two decimal places.

Email			
To:	Credit Controller	**Date:**	Today
From:	AAT Technician	**Subject:**	New Customer Glow Ltd

Please find below my calculations. observations and recommendation for new customer Glow Ltd.

Profitability

The sales revenue has decreased 11.64 % which may be a bad sign. The gross profit margin has reduced from 65.95 % in 20X4 to 56.58 % in 20X5. This means that the selling price has decreased or the cost of sales has increased

The gross profit has fallen in absolute terms by 24.18 %. The most important indicator of profitability is the operating profit margin which has fallen from 17.24 % in 20X4 to −4.39 % in 20X5.

The operating loss has been caused by a combination of the decrease in gross profit and the increase of 10.62 % in combined distribution and administration costs.

Liquidity

The current ratio has fallen from 3.38 in 20X4 to 2.19 in 20X5. This is because there has been an increase in current liabilities and a decrease in current assets. The business still has cash in hand, although this has fallen by 22.17 %. The inventory holding period has improved from   184 days in 20X4 to 174 days in 20X5.

The trade receivables collection period has worsened from   80 days in 20X4 to 87 days in 20X5.The payables payment period has increased from 80 days in 20X4 to 139 days in 20X5.

Gearing

Both long-term and short-term borrowing have increased. The gearing ratio has increased to 71.40 % in 20X5. This may have been as a result of acquiring new plant and equipment.

Recommendation

I recommend that

| we defer the decision and ask for further information about future plans |.

Task 5

(a) **Match each type of claim on the left to the appropriate type of court procedure on the right by clicking on the left box first then on the corresponding right box. You can remove a line by clicking on it**

| **Claim** | | **Court procedure** |

(b) **Which of the following statements are true in the context of bankruptcy and insolvency?**

	True ✓	False ✓
Bankruptcy arises where an individual cannot pay his or her debts and is declared bankrupt.	✓	
Insolvency is where a company cannot pay its debts as they fall due.	✓	
If a trade receivable owes an amount of at least £10,000 a statutory demand can be issued for payment of the amount due within a certain period of time		✓
A statutory demand should be made within four months of the debt. If the debt is older than four months a court has to be contacted to explain the reasons behind the delay.	✓	

(c) **Complete the following sentences.**

WRW is offering [a recourse factoring facility] .

XYZ can borrow: [£ | 1,800,000]

(d) **Which of the following are key necessities for goods under the Consumer Rights Act?**

(i) Of satisfactory quality
(ii) At a reasonable price
(iii) Fit for purpose
(iv) As described

	✓
(i), (iii) and (iv)	✓
(i) and (iii)	
All of the above	
(ii) and (iv)	

(e) **Drag and drop the correct words into the following statement.**

Conditions and warranties are two types of terms within a contact. If one party breaks either of them, the other party can sue for [damages] . If one party breaks a [condition] the other party can choose to void the contract.

Which of the following is the correct definition of a garnishee order?

	✓
An order issued by a High Court entitling the creditor to instruct an agent to collect assets from the debtor.	
An order issued by a court entitling the creditor to enter the premises of the debtor to seize assets to the value of the debt.	
An order issued by a County Court entitling the creditor to instruct a court employee to collect assets from the debtor	
An order issued by a court entitling a credit to collect payment from the customer of their debtor.	✓

Task 6

(a) **Complete the following email.**

Email

To: Sales Staff   **Date:**   Today

From: AAT Technician   **Subject:**   Early Settlement Discounts

Please find below my explanation of how an annual percentage cost of an early settlement discount is calculated.

The effective rate of interest

If a customer pays promptly to take advantage of a 1% early settlement discount, we will receive 99% of the invoice total. This means that the discount we are giving the customer is $\boxed{1.01}$ of the amount they pay us. This is what it costs us to receive the cash earlier than our normal credit terms. It is called the effective rate of interest.

Discount periods

If the normal credit terms require customers to pay within 30 days of receiving an invoice, and the discount applies if the customer pays within 14 days, we are offering the discount in return for paying 16 days earlier than our normal terms. There are $\boxed{22.81}$ discount periods of 16 days in a 365 day year.

Annual percentage cost of the early settlement discount using simple interest rates

The annual percentage cost is found $\boxed{\text{multiplying}}$ by the effective rate of interest and the discount periods in a year. The annual percentage cost of offering 1% discount to customers paying within 14 days rather than 30 days is $\boxed{23}$ to the nearest whole percent. I trust this will help you in any discussions with customers about early settlement discounts.

AAT Technician

(b) **Calculate the compound annual cost of each discount to two decimal places.**

The simple annual cost of the discount is $\boxed{31.04}$ %.

The compound annual cost of the discount is $\boxed{35.97}$ %.

(c) **Which of the following will deteriorate the liquidity of a business?**

	✓
Allowing customers extended credit terms to encourage them to buy more.	✓
Requiring a deposit with orders and settlement upon delivery of goods.	
Paying suppliers after their required date and forfeiting a settlement discount.	
Moving production to a just in time inventory system	

(d) **Calculate expected cash receipts in month 3.**

£	145,760

(e) **Which of the following statements are true in order for Dunit to be able to successfully reclaim VAT on an unpaid debt?**

	✓
The debt must have remained unpaid for four months after the due date.	
Dunit must have made a provision for the unpaid debt	
The claim must be made within three years of the due date of payment of the debt.	
Dunit must already have accounted for the VAT and paid it over to HMRC	✓

(f) **Calculate the amount that Graham should write off as an irrecoverable debt. Ignore VAT. Show your answer to the nearest penny.**

£	19,100

Task 7

(a)

Care needs to be taken here as PYL seems to be a customer who places regular orders and provides Onegym with a substantial part of their sales – a tactful approach is therefore required. The terms of the sale contract need to be reviewed carefully, as well as delivery documentation, as PYL are possibly in breach of contract if the delivery date was part of the agreed terms.

Even though part of the order was delivered on time, the remainder was 14 days late. If Onegym were determined to be in breach of contract, they would be liable for damages. The amount of damages would be determined based on what PYL might have incurred by way of costs or lost revenue as a result of the delay.

It would therefore be preferable to meet with PYL and negotiate some kind of discount for the problems and inconvenience caused. This would avoid any legal costs, maintain customer goodwill and hopefully bring about payment of the outstanding amount less any discount. As PYL has always otherwise paid to terms, there is no reason to make any provision or take other action to collect the debt at this point.

DUU

A receiver will often attempt to reject ROT claims in the first instance therefore Onegym should check what sort of goods they have recently supplied to DUU. If the goods are small items of equipment then the receiver may be correct that it is not possible to identify which have been supplied by Onegym, particularly if they had not been kept separate by DUU. However, it may be possible to identity Onegym's equipment. Therefore if it is cost-effective to pay a visit to DUU's premises, Onegym should send a representative immediately with all relevant documentation.

Onegym has an 'all monies' retention of title clause. This means that it would not be necessary to match any goods unpaid for to specific outstanding invoices. If the ROT clause turns out to be unenforceable, Onegym will be an unsecured creditor of DUU, which means it is unlikely that Onegym will receive much, if any, of the outstanding amount.

A claim should be made on the credit insurance for the amount of £20,000. (Net debt is £35,000/1.2 = £29,167. Maximum claim is lower of £20,000 or 75% × £29,167 = £21,875). A provision should be made for the balance of £9,167. VAT of £5,833 can be reclaimed from HMRC after six months and after the debt has been written off.

JCC

JCC seem to have used a variety of excuse and delaying tactics, while Onegym has done its best to prove the amount owed. The debt is now substantially overdue (payment was due by 30 September, it is now 31 December, so the debt is 90 days old) with no apparent reason, even though JCC are normally slow payers.

A credit control policy is in place to ensure that Onegym does not suffer any unnecessary liquidity problems or unnecessary bad debts. Because there is no business reason for not pursuing the debt in accordance with the credit control policy, Onegym should proceed to instruct a debt collection agency or commence legal action.

Causing 'unpleasantness' is not a sufficient reason for Onegym not to protect its business position. The HR director's personal situation should have no bearing on Onegym's business decisions and she should not use her position as a director to influence how a policy should be applied for her own personal gain.

(b)   ULK

	November £	December £
Opening balance	60,000	52,800
Invoice	36,000	15,000
Credit note	(3,500)	(3,100)
Interest charge	300	0
Closing balance	52,800	(1,200)
Payments received	**40,000**	**63,500**